History of Florida

A Captivating Guide to the People and Events That Shaped the History of the Sunshine State

CAPTIVATING HISTORY

Free Bonus from Captivating History (Available for a Limited time)

Hi History Lovers!

Now you have a chance to join our exclusive history list so you can get your first history ebook for free as well as discounts and a potential to get more history books for free! Simply visit the link below to join.

Captivatinghistory.com/ebook

Also, make sure to follow us on Facebook, Twitter and Youtube by searching for Captivating History.

Contents

Introduction

When Florida is mentioned, it creates a variety of images in people's minds. For some, Florida is a retirement mecca due to its year-round warm weather. Others see magic when thinking of Florida. The magic might be part of a fantasy kingdom or watching rockets launched into space. Pictures of incredible waterways and beaches also often filter through the minds of people. Regardless of how you visualize Florida, its history has created its present offerings of wonder.

St. Augustine was the first permanent European settlement, and it was established in 1565; Plymouth did not occur until 1620. Though Florida had the first settlement, it was actually the last East Coast area to be developed. Florida did not experience explosive growth until the mid-20th century.

Since so much of today's Florida is a result of its development and innovations since the 1950s, it seems like a newer state to many. However, ancient creatures roamed the lands 1.8 million years ago. Though Florida may have been one of the last areas of the early US to have human inhabitants, evidence supports settlements that date back over fourteen thousand years.

Today, many different people groups occupy Florida. This is due to European colonization and the search for the Fountain of Youth. Juan Ponce de León's quest for eternal youth brought him to the shores of Florida. However, hundreds of thousands of Native Americans were already settled in Florida.

The Europeans' arrival set the stage for tumultuous battles for the incredible geography of Florida. During the Age of Exploration, current-day Florida was controlled by the Spanish and the British. Both countries desired Florida for its valuable land. The American Revolution and the Civil War changed the role of Florida and its economy. And with the advent of the railroad, Florida's tourism industry was born.

Immigrants from Cuba and other islands blended cultures with those already living there while retaining their traditions and beliefs. This has created a unique and incredible melting pot, and it allows Florida's history to stand out from the other fifty. Learning more about the history of Florida will help you understand the importance of different areas in the state. In addition, protecting and appreciating the past offers an ability to appreciate the present.

Reading *History of Florida: A Captivating Guide to the People and Events That Shaped the History of the Sunshine State* brings history, the story of all of us, alive.

Chapter 1 – Florida Before the Europeans

Originally, Florida was connected to a string of volcanoes that formed the Caribbean islands. Over millions of years, the volcanoes were engulfed in the waters of the Caribbean. When the sea levels abated, land resurfaced. The land that reemerged was part of today's Florida. Its new configuration now connected Florida to the continent of North America.

Migration of animals and people from other continents and landforms could and did occur. Millions of years ago, well before Florida became a tourist destination, ancient horses and other mammals roamed the land. Evidence supports the theory that the ancestors of today's horses migrated from other continents via the Bering Strait, which connects Alaska and Siberia. With a topography more like Africa, the grasslands and marshes of Florida provided sustenance for the early horses.

When the landscape of Florida evolved, the grasses that the horses relied upon for sustenance were depleted. Wetter climates and more forested areas led to the decline of the first horses in North America. Horses were subsequently reintroduced to Florida by the Spaniards thousands of years later.

Following the migration of the ancient horses, the first people of Florida traversed from Siberia over fifteen thousand years ago. Their journey was thousands of miles long and thousands of years in the making. The Bering Strait, which was part of Beringia, provided the access route for our ancestors. During the Last Ice Age, Beringia was the uncovered ground of the Bering Sea. Considered a land bridge, this one-thousand-mile pathway allowed ancient travelers to continue their trek for new hunting grounds.

Since there are thousands of miles of land between Florida and Alaska, it is believed that Florida was one of the last areas of the United States to become inhabited by people. During the Pleistocene epoch, the Paleo-Indians arrived in Florida. Evidence suggests that these early inhabitants were hunter-gatherers. Thus, they lived a nomadic existence, hunting for food and gathering vegetation. When they depleted their food sources, these early peoples traveled to the next available supply of sustenance. They traversed large areas of land in search of resources and food. Much of the game they hunted are now extinct, such as mammoths and mastodons. Their hunting tools included spears, arrowheads, and knives that were carved from stone and animal bones.

During this time period, lower sea levels created a Florida that was double the size of today's state. A much drier climate and landform dictated the migratory paths of the Paleo-Indians. The rivers, canals, and springs that are part of Florida today did not exist for the ancient inhabitants.

Locations with water drew the Paleo-Indians, and they set up their basecamps there. Due to the difficulty of finding water, it was essential for their survival to prioritize this resource. These sites were also alluring to the animals that the Paleo-Indians hunted.

Due to the changes in topography, these campsites are now part of the floors of rivers and sinkholes. These sites have provided remnants of the tools used by the Paleo-Indians. Artifacts of animal bones exist alongside the tools, which provide support of the traveling pathways and means of sustenance of the original Floridians.

Around 9000 BCE, the glaciers begin melting due to increasing temperatures, causing the sea levels to rise. The Paleo-Indians were experiencing the end of the Ice Age. This resulted in the shifting of their eating and hunting patterns. These ancient people started hunting smaller game and gathering plants, which changed their diet. As more waterways emerged with the climate change, the Paleo-Indians began to fish. Evidence of forming fishhooks from bones and antlers of small game support the evolving hunting and gathering habits of the early Americans. Turtles, manatees, and sharks also acted as food sources.

The transition from the Paleo-Indian Age to the Early Archaic Period occurred around 8000 BCE. Hastening the transformation was an increase in temperatures and precipitation. With more rainfall and water available, the Early Archaic people's way of life continued evolving. They were still hunters and gatherers, but their quarry became smaller game. Vegetation in the area also changed, which impacted their diet. More fruits, berries, and nuts grew, and they were scavenged and eaten.

Although the Early Archaic people remained nomadic, the groups in which they traveled became larger. This is partly due to the fact that the size of Florida was reduced due to the increase in sea levels. The rising levels of water created more ponds, lakes, and rivers, which are all part of Florida today. These waterways became locations for a larger number of base camps. With the increase in access to aquatic resources, marine life and shellfish grew in importance in the diets of the Early Archaic people.

Remains of small game provide evidence of the movements of the Early Archaic people in Florida. Along with animal and shellfish remains, stone and bone tools have also been found. Much of what is known of these peoples come from the Windover Pond site in

Florida. This location, which is about five miles from Cape Canaveral, has provided evidence of the evolution of the formation of tools.

The tools that have been found are more pointed with side notching. The invention of atlatls, which are essentially spear-throwers, demonstrates an adjustment to the changing environment. Hooks or spurs were situated on long sticks to hold darts or sharpened stones. Atlatls would launch the pointed shafts, enabling early hunters to capture food successfully.

In addition to the tools, the bones of over one hundred people were discovered at Windover. The bones have provided information about the challenges of living between 8000 and 6000 BCE. About half of the people in the graves were younger than eighteen when they died. The bones show diseases, malnutrition, osteoporosis, and broken bones, which give scholars and historians a glimpse into the past. The medicinal use of plants to assist the sick and elderly, along with signs of using splints to aid broken bones and amputations, demonstrates the development of society.

Other artifacts show that these early people wove their textiles. It appears the fabrics were used for a variety of purposes, including clothing, bags, and blankets. Additionally, remnants of gourds were found. These were used for storage. Vessels created from turtle shells were found at the site. These containers were used for cooking food and preparing plants for medicinal purposes.

Much of the evidence from Windover is from bogs that were used as graves. Burial sites in the area support the idea that the people transitioned from a completely nomadic way of life to developing a semi-permanent residence. This coincides with the beginning of the Middle Archaic Period. This era spanned from about 6000 BCE to 3000 BCE.

Evidence of how people of this era lived have been found along waterways in current-day Florida, including the St. Johns River. Evidence of midden mounds, which are trash piles of discarded shells and other waste, shows the existence of semi-permanent residences.

With greater and more reliable access to water, the people of the time reduced the distance of their migratory patterns. The Middle Archaic people adapted to the growing diversity in the resources available to them. Coastal waterways were more plentiful, as was the available shellfish and fish life.

Locally available stones were used to create tools and other utensils. In addition, the bones of animals and fish were shaped into useful instruments. Shelters were still made to be temporary because the population, for the most part, was still mobile. Since people did not need to traverse as far for their sustenance, populations grew. Climate conditions continued to evolve, and water overtook what had been open habitats for hunters and gatherers. With a shrinking landmass, the migratory patterns of the Middle Archaic people changed. People became more sedentary. However, much of the evidence of this time period is under the ocean, river, and lake floors.

More remains have been located to gain a clearer picture of the Late Archaic Period (5000 BCE–3000 BCE). People learned to adapt to life near wetlands and along water routes. This is evident in the extensive midden mounds of discarded shells. Fish and shellfish became an increasingly important part of the diet of this time. Sites of this era have been found along the Indian and St. Johns Rivers.

The Late Archaic people built more permanent settlements than the people of previous periods. People no longer had to continually move to find food. Much of the food could be sourced near the settlements that were created. Food and water were now readily available in a smaller geographic area.

The nomadic people's way of life had been based on the climate and adapting to the environment. Since the climate was more stable, this was no longer a challenge for the people's survival. The Late Archaic people could now adapt to their local environment. This caused the development of societies, as groups of people settled near each other.

Social norms were gradually established, with the groups learning to live as neighbors. This caused regions and different areas to develop their own cultures. Some of their societal traditions included cremations with burials of the ashes, with both becoming more prominent during the Late Archaic time. Evidence of mound construction for burial sites emerged in this period. More important people in the settlement were buried in a distinguished mound, which noted their significance in society.

Cultures that began developing during the Late Archaic Period define the next stages in Florida's pre-European history. This is often referred to as the Transitional Period or the Orange Period (3000-500 BCE). Regardless of the terminology used, this era is defined by an increase in social stratification, a more sedentary lifestyle, the cultivation of crops, the creation of ceramics, and population growth.

The adaptation of diets to the food available in the area reduced the necessity to travel far distances as hunters and gatherers. This supported the transition from a nomadic lifestyle, with small groups moving together to semi-permanent structures and forming early villages. Hierarchies within the villages emerged as leaders rose to guide the community. This way of life fostered an increase in the population. These attributes of society link the Late Archaic Period to the Transitional Period.

Key technological advances occurred during the Orange or Transitional Period. These innovations include the introduction and use of ceramics, new tools and weapons, and the cultivation of crops. Early ceramics from the Orange Period were fiber-tempered. Grasses and plants from the St. Johns River area were used as the fiber element in the construction of these ceramics. The earliest ceramic pieces from this watershed area were plain and unadorned.

As the early people developed their skills, pottery was chiseled or engraved, which allowed the vessels to become more ornate. Regional distinctions can be seen in the designs of pottery. Utilizing the rich resources available in the waterways, people infused sand, shells, and limestone in their pottery. The new materials allowed the potters to create stronger vessels. Sand and other materials from the river and its banks were used as the temper in the ceramics, replacing plant fibers.

Atlatls, spear-throwers, which used stone points, were used by the first peoples who arrived in the Americas. These allowed the hunter to be some distance away from their prey. Atlatls are very powerful weapons, which were needed when the early people hunted mastodons, which could be seven to ten feet tall. As the food they hunted changed, tools to hunt successfully had to evolve as well.

During the Transitional Period, evidence of triangular stone projectiles demonstrates the evolution of tools and weaponry. These stone projectiles suggest the bow and arrow was introduced to the area. The bow and arrow would have made hunting deer and small game much easier. In addition to hunting, the bow and arrow was used as a weapon. When the Europeans arrived, which happened about one thousand years after the bow and arrow became part of the weaponry of Native Americans in Florida, the indigenous peoples needed to employ the weapon for protection because of its accuracy.

As people stayed in certain areas and created villages, agriculture became a means to feed a growing population. Since corn can be cooked in a number of ways, it became a staple of the diets of the Native Americans. Corn was frequently grown in concert with beans and squash. Beans were planted near corn stalks, so the stalks could act as a trellis for the beans to grow. Additionally, the corn stalks offered shade for the squash. Native Americans did not grow their food in rows; they employed a system of mounds. Vegetables that complemented each other for support, shade, or nutrients in the soil were grown in the same mound.

The early Native American groups were not called tribes by anthropologists. Rather, they use the word "cultures" to refer to the groups who hunted and gathered together, as well as those who settled in semi-permanent villages. One of the first groups or cultures that embody the Transitional Period in Florida is the Timucua. They were the largest of the indigenous groups of people in northern Florida.

Depiction of Timucua women

As a grouping of separate cultures, they had thirty-five different chiefdoms or political units. These splintered groups were often rivals of each other, and alliances frequently shifted. Though they spoke different dialects of the same language, they did not view themselves as a united group.

Similar to other cultures of the era, the Timucua cultivated their own food. Corn or maize, squash, and beans were an important part of their diet. In addition to growing their own food, they also relied on fishing. The Timucua were talented canoe builders. Evidence of the foods they ate and grew has been obtained by the shell middens that still exist. The sun and the moon were at the center of their religious beliefs. While chiefs had the most power, even in regards to religion, the shamans had special abilities. Shamans could dispense blessings and curses. The Timucua inhabited over 19,000 miles and had a population of over 200,000 when the Europeans arrived.

Apalachee Council House reproduction located in Tallahassee

Living to the west of the Timucua were the Apalachee. They lived on the land between the Ochlockonee and Aucilla Rivers, and they relied on agriculture for their survival. Their land was rich loam, which provided bountiful harvests. Since the Apalachee were so successful with the crops they cultivated, they were one of the largest and most powerful cultures in Florida when the Europeans landed. Part of their success was because they were a very organized culture. Chiefs inherited their positions and were guided in their decisions by priests.

On the southwestern coast of Florida were the Calusa. Their territory contained most of current-day southern Florida. The Calusa relied on the nearby waterways for their food. They made nets from palm tree webbing and used spears to catch fish. They formed canoes from carved-out cypress trees, and they are known to have voyaged as far as Cuba. Much is known about the Calusa from their shell mounds. The Calusa people were a complex and hierarchal society, and they were separated into different groups within their culture. They believed there was life after death, and the Calusa made daily offerings to their dead ancestors.

A museum display of the Calusa

Villages created and inhabited by the Tocobaga were located near Tampa Bay. Like the Calusa, they relied on the bay for much of their food and formed garbage heaps or middens with discarded shells and other waste. The Tocobaga were also hunters since they lived on lands abundant with small game. To distinguish their status within their society, the Tocobaga people used tattoos. They formed many small villages, which each followed the same social structure, with a chief as their leader.

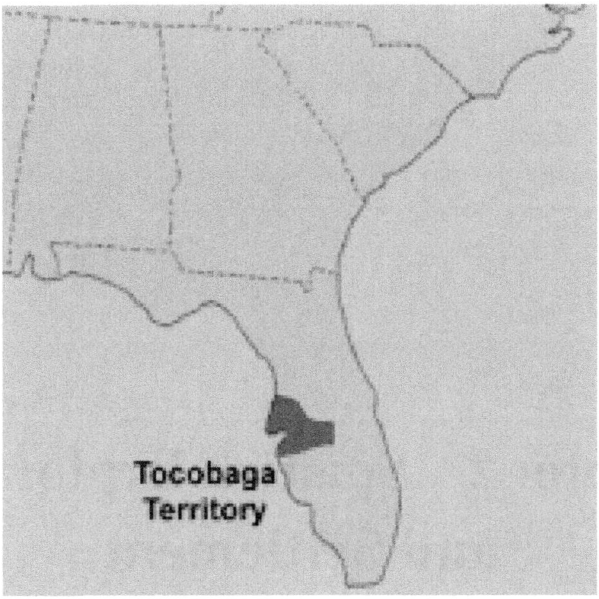

Map of where the Tocobaga settled

From 700 CE until the arrival of the Spaniards, these native cultures evolved and flourished. Complex societies greeted the Europeans when they landed on North American soil.

Chapter 2 – Spanish Exploration and Settlement

As the Spanish, French, and English sought to expand their empires and increase their wealth, Florida became a battleground between the three nations. Indigenous peoples in Florida numbered over 350,000 when the first European explorers arrived. With the arrival of Juan Ponce de León, a Spanish explorer, the landscape of Florida was forever altered.

Juan Ponce de León was part of the group of early Spanish explorers known as conquistadors, or "conquerors," and he was the first to come ashore in Florida. Before this happened, Ponce de León sailed as part of Christopher Columbus's second voyage to the Americas in 1493. Ponce de León stayed with his family on the island of Hispaniola, where he was the military commander and later became the deputy governor.

He continued to explore areas around Hispaniola, seeking gold and other fortunes. One such island was the island of Borinquén, which was home to the indigenous Taíno. Here, Ponce de León discovered significant amounts of gold. Under the directive of the king of Spain, he established the first settlement on the island, which was later renamed Puerto Rico. Ponce de León served as the governor for two years. During that time, Columbus's son, Diego, was fighting for his right to lead Puerto Rico. Diego believed that he was entitled to rule areas that his father had claimed for Spain. He battled in Madrid's courts and eventually won. Therefore, Ponce de León was removed from office. De León refused to work with Diego. Instead, de León sought to restore his good name. The Crown granted him permission to continue his explorations.

Myths surround de León's purposes for his journeys. Many feel he was seeking the Fountain of Youth. Reports about de León's search for the Fountain of Youth were all published after his death. De León did not leave any written evidence saying that he was searching for more than gold. Since de León had married a much younger woman, there was speculation that he wanted to ensure his virility. Thus, according to some, he might have been searching for a magical water source to keep him young. Most records support that de León was searching for lands to colonize and convert to Christianity for Spain. Regardless of his motivations, his quests as a conquistador caused him to sail from Puerto Rico in pursuit of new lands.

A possible landing site of Ponce de León, located near St. Augustine

Supposedly landing near St. Augustine in March of 1513, de León was the first European to step foot on Florida's soil. When he arrived, de León was welcomed by Florida's beautiful flora during the Easter season. He claimed the land for Spain, and he chose Pascua Florida as its name after the Easter Feast of flowers.

His explorations did not end in St. Augustine, though. He continued sailing south. Ponce de León and his crew went ashore when they spotted Native Americans. This occurred near the current-day Daytona Beach area. The Native Americans they saw were likely the Timucua, and the natives protected themselves and attacked the Spaniards with spears and arrows. The Spaniards fought back with their steel swords and guns, which allowed them to escape.

After encountering choppy seas, Ponce de León dubbed his next stop as Cape Canaveral, which means the "Cape of Currents." His next destination was the islands of Dry Tortugas, which he also named. These islands are located about seventy miles west of modern-day Key West. He named the islands this because they did not find potable water on the island; therefore, it was considered dry. They did locate numerous turtles, known as *tortugas* in Spanish.

In 1521, Ponce de León returned to Florida. On this voyage, he was prepared to start a colony for the country of Spain. The Calusa feared that Ponce de León wanted their land. They attacked the colonists, and in the ensuing battle, Ponce de León was struck by a poisoned arrow. This caused Ponce de León and his men to return to their ships and leave Florida. He died from his wounds in Cuba not long after.

Though Ponce de León was not successful in establishing a colony, his exploration paved the way for others. Following Ponce de León was fellow Spaniard Pánfilo de Narváez. De Narváez was charged with establishing two towns and three forts. Seeking to avoid the same fate as de León, de Narváez landed near the Tampa Bay region in 1528. This was about one hundred miles north of where de León encountered the Calusa.

After claiming the land for Spain, de Narváez started inland in his quest for gold. The farther he traversed, the more disoriented he and his crew became. Though he tried to avoid the Calusa, he ended up fighting many skirmishes with them. Gold was never located, and no settlements were ever established. De Narváez and most of his men were lost at sea later that same year.

Hernando de Soto arrived in the Tampa Bay area in 1539 with over one thousand men, women, and priests. He also sailed for the king of Spain, who at this time was Charles I (r. 1516–1556; also known as Charles V, Holy Roman Emperor). With such a large contingent, de Soto needed to continually obtain more food and horses. There were a number of different tribes in the area with whom de Soto traded. However, as a Spanish conquistador known for his brutality, when he was not successful bartering for his supplies, he battled and massacred many of the Native Americans he encountered.

During the summer months, de Soto and his men traveled through Florida in the pursuit of gold. Word of his treatment of the Native Americans preceded him. When they reached central Florida, they came upon an Apalachee village called Anhaica. Scouts had warned the Apalachee of de Soto's cruelty, so the Apalachee had already abandoned the village. Before leaving, the Apalachee destroyed all of their crops. De Soto and his troops used this village during the winter months.

For the next couple of years, his relentless pursuit of gold, silver, and other riches took him throughout much of the southeastern United States. His expedition ended at what became known as the Mississippi River. Here, he contracted a fever and died. It is believed that he is buried on the banks of the great Mississippi.

The monarchy of Spain began to realize that the Spanish conquistadors were not successfully establishing colonies, so it changed its approach. The Spanish Crown still sought to colonize Florida, but this time, missionaries were sent. A Dominican friar named Luis Cáncer de Barbastro, who had other successful missions, was selected to lead this expedition. King Charles I of Spain approved the voyage with the stipulation that the expedition avoid the areas that had been devastated by de Narváez and de Soto.

In 1549, Father de Barbastro's ship landed near the Tampa Bay area, despite the king's warning. Thinking they had encountered Native Americans who would be willing converts, de Barbastro swam ashore. Once he reached the shore, he kneeled in prayer, trying to let the local tribes know his intentions. However, once he stood, de Barbastro was attacked and killed.

A decade later, another Spanish conquistador named Tristán de Luna was called upon by Luís Velasco to establish a chain of colonies in Florida. Velasco, the viceroy of New Spain (Mexico), was seeking the establishment of colonies to provide a stopping point between Spain and Mexico for ships.

De Luna set sail with a large expedition of five hundred soldiers and one thousand settlers. They arrived near present-day Pensacola Harbor. From there, he sent small groups out to establish settlements. Native American encounters were relatively few. The negative toll of battles with previous explorers and the impact of Spanish diseases had dramatically reduced the indigenous people's population.

De Luna's mission was unsuccessful because of poor decisions. For instance, he left the ships loaded with provisions in the harbor, which caused his men to doubt his leadership. A hurricane struck the harbor, destroying the ships and most of the provisions aboard. The soldiers and colonists moved inland and located an abandoned village called Nanipacana. They renamed it Santa Cruz and began to shape it into a more permanent settlement. They survived the winter because of the arrival of relief ships. However, in the spring, more relief did not arrive. Their attempts at planting were not successful, and the settlement was abandoned in 1561.

The Spanish were not the only Europeans interested in the colonization of Florida. The first group from France arrived in 1562. Jean Ribault sailed for France with two purposes in mind. The first was to find a colony in which the Huguenots could settle. The Huguenots were French Protestants who were seeking a spot where they could freely practice their religion. In France, Huguenots were persecuted. Secondly, the French were interested in the response that their arrival would cause with the Spaniards.

After landing near the St. Augustine region, Ribualt had his men build a stone pillar to claim the land for France. The monument was constructed at the mouth of the St. Johns River. They continued north, searching for a good harbor and outpost location. Ribault and his men selected an island off the shore of today's South Carolina. They built a small fort, which he named Charlesfort in honor of King Charles IX of France.

Charlesfort was a short-lived settlement. Ribualt soon returned to France for supplies. Once he arrived, he found France embroiled in a war between the Catholics and Huguenots, so he was forced to seek assistance in England. After arriving in England, he was jailed for his religious beliefs. The settlers who remained at Charlesfort grew concerned when Ribualt did not return.

They constructed a ship that was not well-built. On their journey back to Europe, many died from disease and starvation. The survivors resorted to cannibalism to stay alive.

René de Laudonnière, Ribualt's second-in-command, was commissioned by King Charles IX to lead the next colonization attempt. He sailed with soldiers and colonists who were a mix of different religions, ages, genders, and wealth. Not knowing in what condition he would find Charlesfort, he sailed to the mouth of St. Johns River where the stone pillar was constructed.

At this location, they constructed a triangle-shaped fort that offered protection. Named Fort Caroline, the colony initially seemed successful. They had a peaceful relationship with the Timucua. However, the work was extremely difficult. Laudonnière's leadership was in jeopardy, and he sent the colonists he thought would challenge him back to France.

Part of the Timucuan preserve near Fort Caroline

However, problems continued with shortages of food and supplies. Laudonnière selected colonists who were challenging him to go on exploration missions. Many of these settlers deserted the colony. The deserters, who were in need of food, stole from the Timucua. This caused a deteriorating relationship between the Timucua and the remaining colonists.

Laudonnière and the rest of the colonists began making plans to return to France in 1565. Around this same time, Ribault was being released from prison. King Charles IX sent Ribault back to Florida with the hopes of retaining control of Fort Caroline and maintaining a presence in Florida.

Spain's King Philip II wanted the French threat eliminated. Fort Caroline was seen as a hindrance to Spain's ability to safely run shipments of gold and silver from the New World to Spain. The location of Fort Caroline would have allowed the French access to the Spanish ships. Additionally, Philip was fiercely Catholic, and the settlement was Protestant, which he viewed as an affront.

Now that Ribault was on his way to restore order to Fort Caroline, Philip needed to counter that move. Pedro Menéndez de Avilés was selected to disband the settlement and force the French settlers to return to France.

Menéndez's mission was to eliminate the French Huguenot colonists, as the Huguenots were seeking to assume Spain's claim on the land. Menéndez was essentially racing against the clock. Philip wanted him to destroy the French colony of Fort Caroline before Ribault could lead the charge in saving the colony.

The French fleet arrived before Menéndez, which he discovered when he scouted the fort. Knowing he was greatly outnumbered, Menéndez withdrew to the location he named St. Augustine. Just when the French fleet prepared to attack the Spaniards, a hurricane forced the fleet south.

Menéndez knew that Ribault's ships would need to wait until the storm subsided to try to reach St. Augustine again. He took advantage of this and marched his men through the rains and winds of the hurricane to Fort Caroline. They arrived before dawn and attacked the fort.

Most of the French remaining at the fort were killed. Some escaped to the wilderness; others were captured and hanged. After renaming the fort San Mateo, Menéndez returned to St. Augustine with his troops, expecting to find Ribault and his men. However, the storm had sunk the fleet. Menéndez found Ribault and his men on the beach along the river to St. Augustine. Many of the men were injured by the shipwreck. Menéndez was not able to feed or care for all the survivors, so he chose to execute most of the men. Over three hundred people were killed by Menéndez's soldiers. The river is now called Matanzas, which means "massacre" in Spanish. This devastation ended the idea of French colonies in Florida.

Now that Spain was the controlling European influence in Florida, they readied themselves to accomplish their secondary mission of exploration. Converting Native Americans to Catholicism was considered a means to spread their faith and control the indigenous people. Jesuits, a Catholic order of priests, were sent by the king soon after Menéndez established St. Augustine in 1565. This would be the first permanent settlement in North America, and it has the distinction of being the oldest permanently inhabited settlement of the United States.

The Jesuits' initial attempts to work with local Native Americans were thwarted when one of the first three missionaries was killed. The remaining two Jesuit priests worked near St. Augustine with different groups of Native Americans. Much of their work was focused on translating the Bible. Since they were not attaining conversions to Catholicism as they had wanted, the Jesuits withdrew from Florida and moved their missions to New Spain, which was farther south.

A few years later, the Franciscans, another order of Catholic priests, arrived in Florida. The Franciscans provided gifts to the chiefs and other important leaders. In return, the chiefs would permit the building of a doctrina in their village. Doctrinas were small village mission posts that included a chapel and living quarters for missionaries.

The first two doctrinas were built in 1587 outside of St. Augustine. Gradually, a system of missions was established along the coast and eventually extended west to what is now the Florida Panhandle. A new missionary post would not be built until the previous one was safely and clearly established. No post was more than a one day's ride from the other. This networking system lasted until the early 1700s. At this time, Native American populations were declining. Spain's prominence was also waning, as England and France were asserting their power and control in Europe and the New World.

England had been continuing its expansion of the colonies along the eastern seaboard. This brought the British near the Spanish in Florida. Once the English reached modern-day Charleston, South Carolina, the Spanish began fortifying St. Augustine. Therefore, in 1672, the Spaniards began the construction of Castillo de San Marcos.

Knowing they were vulnerable to attacks from the west, Fort San Marcos de Apalache was built. The location was chosen to protect the mission at San Luis (near modern-day Tallahassee, Florida).

Picture of Castillo de San Marcos

The English governor in Carolina attacked Spanish missions as they proceeded to St. Augustine. The Spanish were able to hold the English invasion off through a war of attrition, and the Spanish governor ordered people and local Native Americans to take shelter in Castillo de San Marcos. They stayed in the fortress for over fifty days. In the end, the English were thwarted, especially when they saw enemy supply ships arrive. Withdrawing from the city, James Moore, an Irish military officer and the governor of Carolina, had his troops burn the city to the ground. As they withdrew back to Charleston, they also burned Native American villages and missions.

Moore was angry over his defeat, and he continued his attacks on the Spanish and Native Americans in Florida. Through a series of attacks during 1703 and 1704 on smaller villages and on the Apalachee missions, he returned to Carolina with four thousand captives, mostly women and children. Many of them were sold into slavery.

Chapter 3 – From Spain to Britain

The British, eyeing full control of Florida, continued to use different Native American tribes to assist them in monitoring the Spanish. Skirmishes between the British and Spanish, with varying combinations of Native Americans, occurred for years. The conflicts between Great Britain and France were also escalating.

France extended their reach on the North American continent with settlements in the Ohio River Valley, which is land that the British claimed. Back-and-forth clashes between the two countries began around 1750. In 1756, Great Britain formally declared war on France. The Seven Years' War, also known as the French and Indian War in the colonies, was partially fought for control of North America.

Early in the war, the British were successfully winning the majority of the battles. This prompted Spain to enter the war on the side of the French in 1760. While the war was not fought on Florida soil, the outcome had a tremendous impact on its future. During the war, Britain captured Havana, Cuba, from Spain. This was perhaps Spain's busiest port in the Americas.

The war ended in 1763 with the Treaty of Paris. As part of the agreement, France had to give Britain its land in today's Canada, although it was allowed to retain its territories west of the Mississippi River. The triumphant British exchanged control of Havana for Florida with the Spanish. The Florida that the British gained was much different than today's Florida. Its land included vastly more than the present-day state. Extending westward to the Mississippi River, it encompassed parts of Alabama, Mississippi, and Louisiana.

Another outcome of the French and Indian War was the Proclamation of 1763. The proclamation stated that the colonists could not settle lands west of the Appalachian Mountains. It also stipulated that only qualified traders could make deals with the Native Americans on behalf of the British Crown. The British had multiple purposes for enacting this declaration. One was to increase their control over the colonists. It was also an attempt to collaborate with the Native Americans and provide land for them since many of them had fought in the French and Indian War.

Additionally, under the Proclamation of 1763, King George III added three new colonies on the North American continent: Quebec, East Florida, and West Florida. East and West Florida were the fourteenth and fifteenth British colonies in what eventually became the United States.

A map of where East and West Florida were divided

Before assuming control of Florida, the British permitted those occupying the territory to leave. Most of the Spanish citizens, freed slaves, and Catholic Native Americans moved to Cuba as part of this agreement. Enslaved people either moved with their owners to Cuba or remained in Florida. The British also created a separate territory in which the Native Americans were allowed to stay. Their area was another provision established under the Proclamation of 1763. New colonists could not settle on this land.

East Florida's capital was established in St. Augustine, and James Grant, a British officer, was chosen as its governor in 1764. He controlled the land that spanned all of the peninsula of Florida west to the Apalachicola River and the Gulf of Mexico. But for the colonies to survive, they needed colonists.

A portrait of James Grant

Governor Grant invited colonists from the Carolinas, Georgia, and other British colonies to move to East Florida to start farms or plantations. To encourage colonists to move from the southern colonies, Grant permitted slavery in East Florida. The land Grant governed was superior farmland. Land grants were created to attract people from Britain. Many of the people who took advantage of the land grants actually stayed in London. Some of these new landowners formed the East Florida Society, and they sought to make profits from their shares of land.

Grant fostered a good working relationship with the Seminoles and encouraged trade that benefited both parties. For years, there was a peaceful coexistence between the settlers and the indigenous people. During this time, conflicts between the settlers and the Native Americans were few. This permitted the British to expand upon the housing in St. Augustine.

Governing West Florida was George Johnstone, an officer of the Royal Navy. His colony began where East Florida ended at the Apalachicola River and extended west along the Gulf of Mexico to the Mississippi River. West Florida was comprised of parts of Alabama, Mississippi, and Louisiana. Pensacola served as its capital. Its land was not as fertile as East Florida, which made attracting settlers seeking land to farm more difficult. Settlers who chose to move to West Florida successfully engaged in fur trading and selling lumber.

Different means of advertising were tried, and they had varying degrees of success. Prior to the American Revolution, East Florida had several thousand inhabitants. West Florida, on the other hand, is thought to have had only several hundred. It is believed neither colony had a large enough population to ensure its sustainability.

However, some parts of the newly formed colonies of East and West Florida were showing signs of achievement. Indigo, which is a plant that creates a blue dye, was thriving in the southern soil. Blue cloth and clothing were in huge demand in Europe. Near St. Augustine, there was available land and housing, and the British settled into the housing left behind by the Spaniards. With Florida's sunshine, British property owners were planting lucrative indigo and other crops.

Ships sailed from St. Augustine loaded with cargos of indigo and lumber harvested from the area. The return ships contained sugar and other goods. British-controlled Florida was beginning to prosper, and the Florida colonists were starting to experience a positive return on their investments in the land.

During the same time, the original Thirteen Colonies began to resent British rule. However, Florida needed the British. They relied on Britain for protection. As rebellion and the anti-tax movement swept the other colonies, Florida continued its allegiance to the motherland. Florida did not participate in the Stamp Act Congress, nor did it send a delegation to the Continental Congress in 1776. Florida did not even receive an invitation to send representatives to the Second Continental Congress.

Floridians did not have the same "no taxation without representation" fervor that the Thirteen Colonies had. The Florida plantations were making money, and they were not being taxed. Part of the deal that Floridian colonists received to encourage settlement and develop sustainable business ventures was no taxes. The British had agreed not to tax the plantations until they were fully profitable.

While many in the Thirteen Colonies cheered upon the signing of the Declaration of Independence, Floridians became concerned about their future. Financially, they relied on trade with the northern colonies. Neighboring colonies were fearful that Florida would ally with the Native Americans and attack Georgia or South Carolina. Loyalists, those who supported the British Crown, from the northern and neighboring colonies sought refuge in Florida.

Florida was a strategic location that the British military relied upon. Many of Britain's forces were in the Caribbean. Sugar produced there was an essential element of Great Britain's economy. So, troops were stationed throughout the sugar-producing islands of the Caribbean to protect the crops.

This put East and West Florida in the middle of where British forces needed to allocate their resources; the Caribbean was to the south, and the thirteen rebelling colonies were directly north of Florida. Great Britain initiated attacks on the colonies from St. Augustine and Pensacola. In return, George Washington, the commander of the Continental Army, ordered five separate invasions of Florida.

Fear of attack by the rebellious colonists remained a worry for residents of British Florida. The Patriots, those who opposed Britain's rule, first planned to capture St. Augustine was enacted in 1777. Rebel troops from Georgia prepared to march through East Florida to St. Augustine, but the troops never reached the Florida border. Communication issues, illnesses, and poor training caused the failure.

General Robert Howe of the Continental Army commanded the next assault on Florida in 1778. Again, his goal was to capture St. Augustine for the Patriots. However, British troops, under the direction of General James Provost, planned a march north from St. Augustine. After receiving valuable information from scouts, Provost was warned of the advance of Howe's troops. At Alligator Creek, Provost waited for the Continental Army.

Provost was able to hold the bridge, and the Continental troops withdrew to Savannah. The British troops returned to St. Augustine, where Provost considered his next move. In January of 1779, Provost executed his plan. He attacked Savannah and controlled the city through the remaining years of the American Revolution.

With Savannah securely under British control, residents of East Florida began to feel some relief in their worries of an invasion. However, West Florida became involved in the American Revolution in 1779. At that point in the war, Spain allied with the rebelling American colonies against the British. Spain was seeking to strengthen its status in the world, but it needed more land if it was to compete with the British for control.

Attacks led by General Bernardo de Gálvez, the captain general of Louisiana, resulted in the capture of six British forts, which were located in West and East Florida, in the first month. The Spanish now occupied Natchez, New Orleans, and Baton Rouge. By March of 1780, de Gálvez reached current-day Mobile, which was part of West Florida at this time. After four days of continual bombardment, the city surrendered to the Spaniards fighting for the Continental Army. From there, de Gálvez proceeded to Pensacola.

After assuming control of West Florida after the French and Indian War, the British reinforced forts and other fortifications to protect Pensacola. Spanish, British, and Patriot forces met in battle for control of West Florida in the 1781 Siege of Pensacola. De Gálvez's first attempt failed when his ship was grounded. On his second attempt, de Gálvez sailed the lead ship, the *Gálveztown,* himself. He succeeded, even though he was told he would not, and he sailed into Pensacola Bay with his fleet. However, this time, de Gálvez was thwarted by a hurricane.

Minor battles ensued during April 1781. De Gálvez received additional troops that bolstered his forces to over 7,500, and he readied for a full-on attack. He fired on Fort George in Jacksonville on May 5th, 1781. Intense firing between both sides resulted. For four days, the fort was pelted with relentless gun and cannon fire. Eventually, the Spanish hit the fort with a cannon shot that caused the fort's wall to collapse.

The Spanish forces opened fire on Fort George with their artillery. The British were forced to capitulate. On May 8th, 1781, General John Campbell surrendered.

The British relinquished control of Pensacola to Spain. All of West Florida was under Spanish control from May 1781 until the end of the war. With the British losing more ground, including Savannah, Loyalists from nearby colonies fled to East Florida. The population of East Florida grew dramatically during the years of the American

Revolution, going from four thousand residents to over seventeen thousand.

The American Revolution ended in April of 1783. It was a monumental moment in history. The Treaty of Paris of 1783, which was signed in September of that year, detailed the agreements reached between the British and the other warring parties. The key negotiators for the Patriots were Benjamin Franklin, John Adams, and John Jay. Significant elements of the treaty required King George III to recognize America as its own country, and Britain had to relinquish control of most of its territory east of the Mississippi River.

However, according to the treaty, East and West Florida were once again under Spanish rule. Additionally, the British were required to pay the Floridians for their lost property. Land in the Bahamas was offered to the settlers, most of whom accepted the agreement.

Loyalists in Florida were shocked that they were now under Spanish rule. They felt that they were not rewarded for their allegiance to Britain. For the second time in history, Spain now controlled Florida. However, its rule would not proceed smoothly. Spain's next issue with retaining control of Florida was the emerging power of the United States. The areas within East and West Florida were valuable to the newly formed country. West Florida also had access to the incredible resource of the Mississippi River.

Another complication that the Spanish would face was the population growth of the neighboring United States. This resulted in the displacement of the Creek Confederacy, who were forced south from the Carolinas and Georgia. As the Creek arrived in Florida, they began assimilating with the Yamasee and Apalachee.

The three tribes developed a settlement south of Gainesville, which they named Cuscowilla. At this location, escaped slaves were welcomed. For survival, the newly formed tribe often raided nearby settlements for cattle and horses. Others in the area called the people living at Cuscowilla Seminoles. The derivation of Seminole might be from the Creek words *Ishti Seminole*, which means "outlaws."

Seminole also might be from the Spanish word *cimarron,* which means wild or free. However the word was formed, the Seminoles were formed from Creeks, Apalachee, Timucua, Calusa, and others. Both definitions fit the emerging tribe, which welcomed the remnants of displaced tribes. The "new" tribe traded with the Spanish for survival. The Seminoles would shape Spain's reign over its territory of Florida.

Chapter 4 – Second Spanish Rule

With the Spanish flag flying over Florida again, the Second Spanish period began. It lasted from 1783 until 1821. As mentioned in the previous chapter, Spain regained Florida as part of the Treaty of Paris that ended the American Revolution. Spain's world power was greatly diminished by this point. The toll of wars and colonial expansion had reduced its treasury and influence.

The Spanish government sent General Vicente Manuel de Zéspedes y Velasco to govern the region, which included East Florida and West Florida. He arrived almost twenty-one years after the Spanish flag was last removed. Zéspedes had a difficult task ahead of him. Both colonies of Florida needed more residents to be a viable settlement.

Although they encouraged the British residents to stay and invited the Spanish who had fled to return, Florida had about two thousand civilians in 1790. To help persuade settlers, Zéspedes offered land grants, tax abatements, and cash to families to start farms in Florida. Furthering his push for settlers, Zéspedes no longer restricted people based on their religion. And slave-owning farmers were also allowed to migrate to Florida.

Additionally, the new governor also had to protect Florida from the newly formed United States. Zéspedes enlisted the support of local Native American tribes. The treaties they made included terms that benefited the Native Americans as well. For instance, the Spanish would supply the Native American nations with arms and ammunition as they fought the US to retain control of their tribal land.

Zéspedes also knew that his colony needed trading partners. Therefore, he encouraged ships from the newly formed United States into his harbor. However, even with all of the governor's efforts, Florida was a weakened colony.

During the First Spanish Rule of Florida, the Spaniards had permitted runaway slaves to live in their colony. Zéspedes sought to continue that policy to increase the population of the colonies. When Zéspedes received complaints from US Secretary of State Thomas Jefferson regarding the Spanish treatment of fugitive slaves, he had to comply, as the increasingly powerful US could now start dictating policy in Florida. Zéspedes agreed to repeal Florida's laws that protected escaped slaves.

In addition to population concerns and pressure from the US government, Zéspedes had to contend with an ill-defined western border. The United States and Spain did not agree on a definitive boundary. Living in the area was a mixed population of Native Americans, escaped slaves, and settlers. The Treaty of Paris, which gave the area to Spain, angered the Creeks, who felt that the land was theirs. Land claims would continue to define the next steps in Florida.

The leaders of the Creeks pleaded their case to the British, seeking assistance. One key leader was William Augustus Bowles. Though he was not actually a Native American, the Creeks permitted Bowles to join them when he was stranded in Pensacola by the British Army during the American Revolution. Bowles had two wives: one was a Cherokee, and his other wife was a Creek. For years, Bowles worked to create an Indian Nation.

After being rebuked by the British, Creek leader William Bowles declared their land as the State of Muscogee. Both the Creeks and Seminoles resided in the new state. Bowles again met with the British, offering the allegiance of his people. This gained the attention of the United States and Spain, as neither country wanted Britain involved in their affairs.

The US sent an envoy named Benjamin Hawkins to meet with Bowles. The meeting was a ruse; Hawkins had Bowles arrested. Hawkins released Bowles to the Spanish in exchange for a number of goods and money. They imprisoned him in Havana, and Bowles died there in 1805.

Since the residents of West Florida were still disenfranchised, they were dissatisfied with their Spanish-appointed governor. Charles Delassus led a corrupt regime. Delassus's government was run inefficiently, which allowed dishonest officials to rule. The unscrupulous government official threatened to destroy the prosperity of the colonists. Therefore, the colonists sought reforms and demanded a voice in how they were governed.

However, the colonists were tricked by Delassus, who only pretended to support their insistence on an active role in governing the region. Therefore, in 1810, led by a veteran of the American Revolution, General Philemon Thomas, settlers in the region stormed the Spanish fort of San Carlos in Baton Rouge. After capturing the fort, West Floridians declared independence. With this acquisition, they decreed their lands to be the Republic of West Florida.

Soon after their independence, the residents requested annexation by the United States. This request was posed to the governors of present-day Louisiana and Mississippi. However, both governors were uncertain of their roles and did not immediately respond. They asked for guidance from the president. Residents of the new republic moved ahead with establishing their new country. On October 24th, 1810, the constitution was approved. St. Francisville in today's Louisiana was made the republic's capital, with Fulwar Skipwith as its leader.

Three days after the constitution was approved, US President James Madison annexed the short-lived republic. Troops from the United States raised the Stars and Stripes over Francisville in December 1810. Buoyed by this revolution, in 1811, President James Madison developed a plan to take over East Florida. This secret plan manifested itself as the Patriots' Rebellion.

Patriots who were living in East Florida attempted to overthrow their government. This was all covertly supported by the United States. The Patriots were joined by armed farmers from Georgia. These farmers had been promised two hundred acres of land in Florida as a reward for a successful attack. But although they destroyed plantations, their attack was not successful. The US government disavowed any knowledge of the plan. President Madison did not want to be drawn into a war with Spain over the acquisition of East Florida.

However, President Madison's quest to gain full control of East Florida led to a joint resolution by Congress on January 15th, 1811. It permitted the development of a secret plan to usurp East Florida from Spain. Madison proposed this plan under the guise of the anarchy that he claimed reigned in the territory.

Looking to assert more pressure on Spain to relinquish control of East Florida, General George Mathews attacked in 1811 as part of Madison's plan. His goal was to take control of St. Augustine. However, his armament was not able to penetrate the fortifications of St. Augustine or Castillo de San Marcos. Spain continued to hang on to its weakening control of Florida.

The mix of population and disagreements over the land were contributing factors to the Patriots' Rebellion or the Patriot War. It was fought during the years of 1812 to 1814 in East Florida. The Patriot War is often viewed as part of the US expansionist efforts, a component of the War of 1812, and/or Georgia's desire for more land. Regardless of the lens, this conflict impacted Floridians and Native Americans.

Upon the start of the War of 1812, President Madison withdrew his clandestine plan so he could focus on his war with Britain. Great Britain had placed trade restrictions on the United States, which proved to be a key factor in the declaration of war. Some in the US viewed this as the "Second War of Independence." However, many, especially in the New England region, did not support the conflict.

Spain was concerned with how the War of 1812 would affect it and Florida. It feared that Great Britain would use this opportunity to control Florida again. If the British commanded Florida, they would be able to use that as a base. From this position, the British could have Native Americans fight for them and raid American settlements.

Also encouraging the strife between tribes was Tecumseh, who wanted the Americans to leave Native American lands. Tecumseh encouraged the Creeks to rebel, but not all of the Creeks agreed with this. Many thought it would be best to open up relationships with the Americans in hopes of gaining better land and trade deals. The Creeks began to split apart, with the warlike faction who were opposed to American settlement being called the Red Sticks. Internal conflict sprang up, with the Red Sticks murdering other Creeks and destroying property.

This was known as the Creek War (1813–1814), and it is seen as an extension of the War of 1812. The Spanish and the British even ended up becoming involved, as they supplied the Red Sticks with weapons. They believed that by arming the warlike faction of the Creeks, they could prevent US expansion. Eventually, the Red Sticks ended up being defeated by General Andrew Jackson in the Battle of Horseshoe Bend. Although many of the Creeks were not Red Sticks, the treaty they were forced to sign did not recognize this; they lost almost all of their remaining land in Georgia and Alabama. Many of the Upper Creek fled to Florida.

The War of 1812 ended in 1815 with the Treaty of Ghent. For the most part, the treaty called for a return to the status quo before the war. However, Native Americans were not able to return to the lands that they held before the War of 1812. This was because many of the tribes had supported the British, although the dreams of US expansion also played a role in this decision. The Native Americans were hopeful that Great Britain would include recognition of Native Americans in the treaty. And while an "Indian barrier state" was brought up, the British did not push for it. They also could no longer support the Native Americans monetarily or with weaponry.

When Britain controlled Florida, they supported the Seminoles, who pushed back on American encroachment on Seminole land. This, combined with the abandonment of Native Americans in the Treaty of Ghent, caused new conflicts to arise. Additionally, Native American tribes in the South, especially the Creeks and Seminoles, had welcomed runaway slaves into their society. After the War of 1812, slave owners entered Florida to search for runaway slaves. The United States Army supported the slave owners, and it assisted the owners in trying to locate runaway slaves.

Americans and Seminoles disagreed over this issue. United States leaders wanted to return Seminoles of African descent to slavery. The Seminoles refused; this eventually led to the First Seminole War (1816–1819). Although the land was controlled by Spain, Andrew Jackson led American soldiers into Florida to fight the Seminoles.

Spain's ineffectual control over its land concerned the United States, as it had led to local rebellions. Once in Florida, Jackson wrote to President James Monroe, suggesting that his mission would be bolstered if he were to take full control of Florida. Jackson's initial steps to assume power over Florida began with the Battle of Negro Fort. This battle was waged in July of 1816, and it was a precursor to the First Seminole War, which took place from 1817 to 1819.

Negro Fort was built during the War of 1812 by the British. After that war ended, African Americans who had been attached to the British Royal Marines remained in the area. The fort housed former slaves and enslaved people seeking freedom. This angered slave owners in Georgia. Andrew Jackson viewed gaining control of this fort as a means to garner support for his desire to dominate Florida.

General Jackson established Fort Scott as his base to attack Negro Fort. Provisions for his forts needed to pass by Negro Fort on the Apalachicola River. There is speculation that Jackson engineered a meeting of two boats from Fort Scott on the river in front of Negro Fort. Known as the Watering Party Massacre, American troops who stopped to refill their water supplies were attacked on the river by troops from Negro Fort.

Using this perhaps planned encounter as justification, Jackson received support to launch his assault on Negro Fort. Leaders of Negro Fort were asked to surrender before the attack commenced. Garson, Negro Fort's leader, replied that he had orders to defend the fort for the British and flew the Union Jack.

Fighting and firing of cannons commenced. US Brigadier General Edmund Gaines led the Americans. A hot shot, which is round shot that is heated until it is red hot, was launched at the fort. The cannonball hit the ammunition storage facility. The sounds of the explosion could be heard over one hundred miles away in Pensacola. Negro Fort was annihilated; 270 people were killed, and all the survivors were injured.

With the directive to recapture escaped slaves, Jackson sent over three thousand troops into Florida in 1817. Encounters with Seminoles on Lake Miccosukee and along the Suwannee River resulted in the destruction of Seminole settlements. Continuing his push into Florida, in 1818, Jackson burned villages and gained control of St. Marks (San Marcos de Apalache). These assaults on Spanish-controlled forts were part of his search for escaped slaves who might have been living among the Seminoles. As a result of Jackson's pursuit, many Seminoles were pushed farther south into Florida.

As part of his campaign, Jackson seized control of Pensacola. The Spanish expressed their outrage. They insisted that Jackson and his troops be removed from Florida and punished for his actions. US

Secretary of State John Quincy Adams denied their demands, despite the fact he was already involved with negotiations to buy Florida from Spain. Instead, Adams issued Spain two alternatives. They needed to control their territory with sufficient troops or relinquish the territory to the United States. An ever-weakening Spain had no choice but to negotiate with US Secretary of State Adams. Foreign minister Luis de Onís advocated for Spain. Their meetings resulted in the Adams-Onís Treaty of 1819.

As a result of the treaty, Spain relinquished control of East Florida to the United States. In addition, Spain agreed that they did not have any claim on West Florida. In return, the United States would pay five million dollars for the damage caused by US citizens who revolted against Spain. The United States and Spain also agreed on the western boundary of the Louisiana Purchase. In addition, Spain needed to forfeit its claim to the Pacific Northwest territory. In exchange, the United States recognized Spain's authority over Texas.

Once control of Florida was assumed by the United States, President Monroe asked Andrew Jackson to be its first governor. Jackson resigned from the army to accept the position. The official transfer of the territory from Spain to the United States occurred on July 17th, 1821, with Jackson officiating the exchange. The US flag was erected over the former Spanish territory when Governor Jackson took office.

Jackson's term as governor was brief. His rule was autocratic; therefore, many residents of Florida were displeased with his tenure. He also disagreed with the members of the Spanish transitional government.

However, Jackson was efficient in setting up a new government. Within weeks, he had Florida's administration operating. He renamed West Florida, now calling it Escambia County. East Florida was called St. Johns County. Within both counties, Jackson also formed a county court system. The courts were located in Pensacola for Escambia

County and St. Augustine for St. Johns County. Additionally, Jackson nominated mayors for both cities.

Once Jackson set up the strong foundation for a state government, he wanted to leave the role. He was missing the involvement he had at the national level. Also, his wife's health was adversely affected by Florida's weather and swamps. In December of 1821, he resigned from the office of governor. Jackson returned to Washington and began his bid for the office of the president of the United States.

Chapter 5 – Territory and Statehood

William Pope DuVal was appointed as the second governor of Florida, and he led the territory from 1822 until 1834. His tenure included the development of Florida's economy, the founding of the new territory's capital, and managing disputes between settlers and Native Americans. DuVal was first appointed by President James Monroe, and he was reappointed by Presidents John Quincy Adams and Andrew Jackson.

DuVal was an effective lobbyist for his territory. He also worked diligently for Native Americans. While he was governor, there were no major rebellions or conflicts. Most of the tribes trusted him to represent them. While DuVal was governor, he treated the Native Americans with respect. His interactions with the tribes were open and honest.

During DuVal's time as governor, the capital of the territory had to be selected. Initially, East and West Florida each had their own capital. In 1824, Tallahassee was selected to be the capital of the entire territory. It was chosen because it was located halfway between St. Augustine and Pensacola. It remains Florida's capital to this day.

Tallahassee is located on the site that once was the capital of the Apalachee. Their capital city was called Anhaica. The area around Tallahassee was prime agricultural land. Settlers were drawn to its fertile soil, as it was ideal for growing cotton. A flourishing plantation economy centered on enslaved people working the fields developed around the territory's capital.

Florida was quickly establishing itself as a part of the southern colonies. Its reliance on an agricultural society defined Florida initially as a United States territory and for years after. Cotton plantations created a group of politically powerful and wealthy landowners. The culture of cotton established many of the social norms and hierarchy structures.

Shopkeepers, artisans, and builders formed the middle class of Florida's society. Small and subsistence farmers, as well as people who tended livestock, were considered lower class. Black people and enslaved peoples had the lowest status in the new Territory of Florida. (Florida gained its territorial status in 1822.)

Plantation life was highly structured for the owners and the workers. From sunrise until sundown, there were chores and tasks that needed to be accomplished daily. Most plantations operated in a similar manner and were constructed in like fashion.

People who engaged in the non-plantation lifestyle were typically located in the sparsely populated areas of the territory. Immigrants from Scotland and Ireland settled on land outside of middle Florida. The land's soil was not as rich as the plantations, but this land was less expensive. People on these farms were frequently referred to as Florida Crackers. They were so named because of the sound of the whips driving mule teams and possibly because of the hardtack (a hard biscuit or cracker) they ate.

These farmers were proud of their accomplishments. Though they worked hard, they were poor. Weekly trips to the county seat for provisions were the biggest source of entertainment. Religion and the Bible were of great importance to these early settlers.

While Florida was being settled and developed by non-natives, the indigenous peoples were losing their lands. Settlers were arriving from the north and taking the land around Tallahassee. Before the influx of other colonists, this land was a Seminole settlement. This, in turn, caused skirmishes between the settlers and Seminoles. The governor asked the Seminoles to move from their land, but his request was refused.

In September 1823, the Seminoles and US government representatives met. The Seminoles were represented by Neamathla; Governor DuVal and a diplomat named James Gadsden spoke for the government. The Seminoles realized that after the Adams-Onís Treaty, they needed some type of protection. DuVal offered the Seminoles an agreement: the Treaty of Moultrie Creek.

The accord required the Seminoles to move south and vacate their land. Also, the Seminoles were to stop assisting and harboring runaway slaves. In exchange, the Seminoles would receive four million acres of land. The land was located south of current-day Ocala, which is in northern Florida. Additionally, the US would assist with money and necessities to facilitate the relocation.

The treaty stipulated that White settlers could construct roads on the reservation. Settlers could also access the reservation to search for runaway slaves. Some of the existing Seminole villages that were located on the banks of the Apalachicola River could remain.

Neither side fully executed their part of the agreement. The reservation did not suit the needs of the Seminoles, as they were not able to herd and plant as they previously did. Money from the government was not promptly provided. As a result, an increase in the skirmishes between the settlers and the Seminoles resulted. Acts of violence committed by the settlers went unpunished.

Nine years later, a new treaty was proposed with the United States, with James Gadsden as the negotiator yet again. The Treaty of Payne's Landing required the Seminoles to move to the territory west of the Mississippi River. This move would be made with the Creeks; in essence, it was asking the Seminoles and Creeks to merge and become one tribe. According to this treaty, the Seminoles could not bring any African Americans; they were to be left behind as slaves.

This treaty came shortly after President Jackson signed the Indian Removal Act, which was passed in 1830. Under the act, all Native Americans who lived east of the Mississippi River were required to vacate their land and move west of the Mississippi. Each tribe would work with the government to negotiate specific details.

The Seminoles were very familiar with Jackson and his tactics. They knew that the president did not see them in a fair light as they had once fought, and they knew their chances for a reasonable treaty were minimal. The Treaty of Payne's Landing essentially nullified the Treaty of Moultrie Creek. Seven Seminole chiefs signed the Treaty of Payne's Landing, but they later denied ever signing it; some even claimed they had been forced to do so. They were not going to leave without a fight.

The treaty stipulated that the Seminoles needed to move within three years. Although the treaty was only ratified in 1834, the US government considered the beginning of the three years to have started when it was signed in 1832. In 1835, the United States Army arrived in Florida to enforce the removal of the Native Americans. Major Francis Dade led his troops from Fort Brooke in Tampa to Fort King in Ocala, but he was ambushed. Osceola, a Seminole warrior, was supposed to lead the surprise attack on the American soldiers. However, he never showed up, as he was preoccupied with a different attack, one that saw the death of Wiley Scott, the US representative from Georgia. The 180 Seminoles attacked anyways, leading to what is now referred to as the Dade massacre. Of the 110 US soldiers, only three survived.

Portrait of Osceola

A few days later, on December 31st, 1835, General Duncan Clinch led another attack. He and his troops were also ambushed. They withdrew from the battle, which took place by the Withlacoochee River.

The Seminoles continued their attacks in 1836. The US Army was struggling to defend itself, and it was not making much progress in its mission of getting the Seminoles to move. Jumper, Alligator, Micanopy, and Osceola led the Seminole contingent, which consisted of about three thousand warriors. They were pitted against an army of more than thirty thousand. Throughout 1836, the undermanned Seminoles attacked plantations in Florida, cut off supply lines, and attacked US forts.

However, things began to change when General Thomas Jesup was assigned to deal with the Second Seminole War in 1836. Jesup sent small groups of his troops to track and attack the Seminoles. This effective strategy resulted in a truce in October 1837. However, the truce was a trick, and Jesup captured Seminole leader Osceola, along with many of his supporters.

Two Seminoles joined forces to create havoc with insurgent-style warfare. Wild Cat or Coacoochee and John Horse or John Cohia directed movements of Seminole families to keep them away from American troops. In the same year, American soldiers captured Coacoochee and John Cohia, along with ten other Seminoles. They escaped from Fort Marion and rallied others to support them.

Colonel Zachary Taylor and over one thousand troops hunted them. The Seminoles evaded the soldiers and went to Lake Okeechobee. Taylor's forces pursued them. Although the Seminoles were severely outnumbered, they managed to inflict heavy losses on Taylor's troops. Eventually, the Seminoles were forced to retreat.

The last significant battle of the Second Seminole War occurred at Loxahatchee River in January 1838. Led by Lieutenant Levin Powell, the US Army confronted a large contingent of Seminoles. The Seminoles successfully held their ground, forcing Powell's troops to retreat. Jesup returned to the same area a few days later. He and his troops suffered the same defeat.

After the Battle of Loxahatchee River, Jesup petitioned the United States government to end the war. He requested that the Seminoles be permitted to live in the Everglades region of Florida. His petition was denied.

For the next few years, the war continued. Small skirmishes, although there were notable events, such as the Harney massacre and Harney's later retribution against the Seminoles. Many Seminoles did move west and joined the Creeks. Between a few hundred and 1,500 Seminoles remained by the time the Second Seminole War was declared to be over on August 14th, 1842.

In the same year, the US government passed the Armed Occupation Act. This act was to encourage White settlement in Florida, further driving Native Americans off their land. Once settlers moved to Florida, they were required to plant on five or more acres of land. The settlers needed to stay there for five years and grow crops. After doing this, they would receive 160 acres of land. In addition, they were provided one year's worth of food. All of this came from the federal government for free to those willing to live on and work the land.

The Second Seminole War cost the US government over twenty million dollars. More than 1,500 soldiers died, and it is unknown how many civilians and Native Americans perished. Tricks and subterfuge by the government harmed its relationship with the Native Americans relationship, and the distrust is still felt to this day.

The Third (and final) Seminole War lasted from 1855 to 1858. It arose due to the continued mistreatment of the Seminole people. This war was mainly fought as a series of small battles, and it resulted from the government's continued pursuit of the Seminoles who remained in Florida. Military patrols were vigilant in seeking Seminoles to capture. Rewards were also issued for the successful seizure of Native Americans.

The war is also referred to as Billy Bowlegs' War. He was one of the last Seminole leaders who refused to move. Wild Cat even tried to convince him to move voluntarily, but he would not budge.

Portrait of Billy Bowlegs

Although there was less violence in this war than the previous one, blood was shed all the same. In May 1858, it was believed the Seminoles in Florida numbered around one hundred, and the war ended. Billy Bowlegs had even agreed to migrate after being paid a large sum to do so. A small group of Native Americans, led by Sam Jones, were some of those who remained in Florida. They hid in the Big Cypress Swamp. Many of the Seminoles in Florida today are descendants of Sam Jones and his band.

While battling the Native Americans, many in Florida were working toward statehood. To be considered for statehood, a territory needed sixty thousand people. In 1837, Florida only had forty-eight thousand people. Though they did not have a sufficient number of people at the time, it would still take years for their statehood to be realized anyway, which gave their population time to grow.

In 1837, Floridians voted on whether or not to pursue the steps to statehood. A narrow margin of voters supported becoming a state. The majority of the residents in central Florida wanted to join the Union. East Florida wanted to wait until the population increased significantly, as it wanted Florida to be admitted as two states. Some residents in West Florida preferred to become part of Alabama.

With a slight majority victory, Florida's next step was to craft a state constitution. Florida held a constitutional convention, which had fifty-six delegates in attendance, in 1839. In their first constitution, Florida was to have an elected governor who would serve a four-year term. In addition, there would be an elected legislature. Slavery would be permitted, and the state would be required to establish a public school system.

Florida's constitution was sent to the US Congress for approval. Since Florida petitioned to join the Union as a slave state, their request was not acted upon for years. The Missouri Compromise, the guideline Congress had to follow, required a balance of slave and free states. Until there was a territory seeking statehood as a free state, Florida had to wait.

Once a territory becomes a state, residents are able to elect their own governors. When an area of land is considered a territory, the governor is appointed by the US president. States are also represented in Congress, which means the people of the state are able to elect senators and representatives to voice their needs.

Eventually, Florida was admitted to the United States of America as the twenty-seventh state, and it became a slave state. Florida's date of statehood is March 3rd, 1845, when President John Tyler signed the bill. Iowa's admittance to the Union was delayed due to boundary disputes. Once those were resolved, Iowa's state convention resubmitted their request for statehood. On December 28th, 1846,

President Polk signed the bill confirming Iowa as a free state to continue the balance dictated by the Missouri Compromise.

William D. Moseley was elected as Florida's first governor. Moseley worked on supporting the growth of agriculture. Florida farmers enjoyed bountiful crops of citrus and cotton, so these were the areas he focused on. As the constitution required, Governor Moseley created state-funded public education. Lastly, he supported the construction of a new state capitol building, which was completed during his tenure.

Portrait of William D. Moseley

Now that Florida was a state, they could elect their first United States senators. David Yulee and James Westcott Jr. were the first senators sent from Florida to Washington, DC. Both remained in public office after their terms as senators. Yulee represented Florida in the Confederate States Congress, although some sources dispute this. After the Civil War, Westcott became Florida's attorney general.

Chapter 6 – Florida in the Civil War

Division in the country had been growing for decades. There were many disagreements over what role the federal government should have in state matters. In particular, the states were divided on the issue of slavery. Many political leaders watched the presidential election of November 6th, 1860, with intense interest.

Abraham Lincoln's election to the presidency of the United States was a pivotal event in Florida's history and that of the whole country. Lincoln did not support the continued spread of slavery in any new territories or states. He hoped that slavery would eventually end in the South, although, at the beginning of his term, he was not seeking to completely eliminate the practice.

Many states wanted to make their own decisions on issues such as slavery. Lincoln's election caused the Southern states to consider taking actions to ensure their ability to govern themselves. Southern governments felt that the state governments should be stronger than the federal government. When states freely joined the Union, it was understood that states could freely leave the Union.

The Union changed dramatically after Lincoln's election. A little more than one month after the people voted, South Carolina announced that it would secede from the Union. This meant that it no longer recognized the United States federal government as its leader. South Carolina did not need to follow the laws of the country; instead, it would govern itself.

Florida, which had been admitted to the Union as a slave state just fifteen years earlier, had an important decision to make. No Floridians had voted for Lincoln. After the election, Governor Edward Perry called for a Secession Convention to meet. He recommended that Florida secede from the Union.

On January 3rd, 1861, the convention was held in Tallahassee. Residents in Florida's thirty-six counties were represented at the convention by sixty-nine delegates. All of the delegates were White males, which is unsurprising given the time period. However, they all owned slaves. And, again, unsurprisingly, almost all of them supported secession. Their discussion focused on the timing to withdraw from the Union. The convention met for seven days, with many people attending to listen to speeches.

Delegates voted on the Declaration of Causes for Seceding on January 10th. Their reasons to leave the Union all centered on slavery. When the vote was tallied, sixty-two delegates voted in favor of seceding, while seven were opposed. Florida was now independent.

Florida was the third state to leave the Union, following in the footsteps of South Carolina and Mississippi. Florida's independence was short-lived. By February of that year, seven Southern states, including Florida, formed the Confederate States of America. Within a month, four other states joined the Confederacy. Mississippi Senator Jefferson Davis was elected provisional president of the newly formed republic.

Florida's decision and that of other Southern states propelled the United States toward a civil war. Mounting disagreements between the states shattered the Union. On April 12th, 1861, Confederate forces fired upon Fort Sumter, which was the first battle of the Civil War. For over four years, brothers fought brothers, and cousins fought cousins. At the end of the war, between 620,000 and 850,000 people had died.

Compared to the other Southern states, Florida had a fairly smaller population. Despite this, Florida supplied the highest percentage of men of fighting age compared to other Confederate states. By the end of the war, over fifteen thousand troops represented Florida in their fight against the Union. Of the fifteen thousand, five thousand soldiers perished. Troops from Florida fought in some of the most significant battles of the Civil War.

While most of the battles were fought in other states, Florida did play an active role in the Civil War. Two battles of significance and a number of smaller clashes occurred on Florida's soil. The length of Florida's coastline also permitted smaller ships to evade the Union's blockade of its larger seaports. These ships could then provide supplies to Confederate troops. Florida also played a significant role in supplying food for the Confederacy.

In the early days of secession, Fort Pickens had the potential to be the initial battle of the Civil War. Fort Pickens, which is on Santa Rosa Island near Pensacola, had US Army soldiers stationed there. Once Florida left the Union, these soldiers were now the enemy.

Engraving of Fort Pickens

Demands made to the Union soldiers to vacate the fort went unheeded. Secessionist troops tried to gain control of the fort without firing a shot, but they were not successful. The Union knew it needed to maintain a foothold in Florida, so the soldiers received reinforcements. A stalemate between the forces lasted for months.

In October, Confederate forces made another attempt to seize the island. One thousand troops stormed the fort. The Union once again sent in more troops. Minor battles occurred on the island throughout the next year. By May of 1862, Confederate forces withdrew their troops from the area. Fort Pickens and Pensacola remained under Union control for the entire war.

Another altercation took place on Florida soil. This is known as the Tampa Incident. In June 1862, a Union ship arrived in Tampa Bay, and the soldiers went ashore. Once in town, the Union troops demanded that Tampa surrender. The Osceola Rangers, a Confederate militia group based in Tampa, refused to do so.

The Union soldiers returned to the ship, and their gunboat fired upon the town. The Union general eventually stopped the firing, but he made sure the Confederates knew that the firing would commence later in the day, giving them time to either surrender or remove their civilians. He was not bluffing, as gunfire later rang out from the boat and continued throughout the next day. The Osceola Rangers persisted in their protection of Tampa Bay. After realizing that the militia group would not surrender, the gunboat withdrew from the harbor.

One of the Civil War's bloodiest battles happened on Florida's soil. On February 20th, 1864, the Union launched an expedition with three main goals. One of the objectives was to cut off supply lines to the Confederacy. Their second objective was to find recruits for the Union; in particular, they sought formerly enslaved people to join the Union ranks. Lastly, the Union forces were hoping to establish a pro-Union government in eastern Florida.

Brigadier General Truman Seymour led the Union forces in the Battle of Olustee. He paraded his troops toward the capital of Tallahassee. In an effort to thwart their advances, Confederate General Joseph Finegan aligned his troops at Olustee. Each side had more than five thousand troops, making this the largest battle fought in Florida.

Battle of Olustee *by Kurz and Allison*

Though it lasted only six hours, almost three thousand men were killed. Finegan's positioning of his troops provided an advantage for the Confederates, as the placement of his troops forced the Union to commit more men in each wave of the battle. In the end, the Union forces withdrew to Jacksonville, delivering a victory for the Confederates. This victory ensured that central Florida remained under the command of the South.

Another venture to access central Florida took place in March 1865. After sailing to the mouth of the St. Marks River, Major General John Newton's troops disembarked at its lighthouse. The Union soldiers marched inland. It is not known if their target was the fort at St. Marks or if they were pursuing Florida's capital city.

Since there was such a large contingent of troops, the Confederate forces believed that Tallahassee was in danger. So, they acted and burned a bridge that prevented the Union troops from crossing the river. The Union troops were not deterred, though. They marched under cover of darkness, seeking to reach Natural Bridge. Confederate scouts detected the movement of the troops, and forces were sent to challenge the Union men.

Early the next morning, the Union troops attempted their river crossing. The Confederate leader, General Sam Jones, and his troops protected all of the access points to the bridge. The battle lasted most of the day. After realizing that the Confederates held a stronger defensive stance, had more firepower, and had more troops, the Union forces retreated. Their ships were still at the mouth of the river, which offered them a safety net.

The Confederates were victorious. Tallahassee was only one of two Southern capital cities that the Union did not capture.

The battles fought in Florida did not decimate the towns and cities, which was what happened in many other states. The Union forces controlled many of Florida's coastal towns; however, the interior lands of the state were part of the Confederacy for the duration of the war.

One way the Union attempted to control the Confederacy was by blockading their ports. Florida's natural harbors proved essential in the importation and exportation of arms and other goods for their new republic. Due to Florida's lengthy coastline, the Union Navy did not have a sufficient number of ships to realistically patrol its shoreline.

Blockade runners successfully evaded Union ships, and these merchant vessels brought war supplies into Florida. These ships frequently sailed from the Caribbean islands. In exchange, cotton, molasses, and whiskey were exported.

As the Union Navy grew, it was able to mount successful campaigns against the blockade runners. The East Gulf Blockading Squadron served as the Union Navy's prime weapon against blockade runners. It was headquartered in Key West, which remained under Union control for the entire war. With more ships and experience, the Union Navy began to make an impact on the supply chain of the Confederate States.

One of Florida's key contributions to the Confederacy was supplying food. Since the Confederates were able to protect the interior lands of the state, farms and plantations continued to raise much-needed food. Florida supplied many crops, including corn and fruit. Beer, pork, and fish were also provided to the troops.

Additionally, Florida produced salt. The state had plants that separated salt from seawater. Seawater was boiled in very large kettles, which caused the water to evaporate and the salt to remain. Florida's two largest salt factories were located at Apalachee Bay and St. Andrews Bay. Refrigeration had not yet been created. So, salt was essential in keeping meats from spoiling.

While large-scale military invasions into northern and central Florida were not feasible by the Union Army, smaller incursions and raids were attempted. To protect the food supply, salt production, and flow of goods in and out of Florida, the "Cow Cavalry" was formed.

These small militia units were usually formed by ranchers and cowhands to initially protect their cattle. This was because the Union forces' first attempted raids were to capture cattle. Then the Union Navy engaged in incursions, seeking to disrupt operations at salt plants. The Cow Cavalry worked to protect Florida's assets and contributions to the war effort.

Since these encounters were not documented, the number of confrontations is unknown. However, since Florida was able to keep supplies flowing, the members of the Cow Calvary must have made a positive impact on the Confederacy's war effort.

Battling against a much larger Union Army was taking a toll on the Confederate States, though. In 1863, President Lincoln signed the Emancipation Proclamation. This freed all enslaved people in the states that had seceded. For Southerners, this had an adverse effect on their morale. Additionally, many freed slaves joined the Union Army to assist in fighting for freedom for all enslaved people.

The war continued for two more years, during which time the Confederacy continued to decline. By the spring of 1865, the end of the war was in sight. The Union had captured many key Southern cities and state capitals. Supplies to Confederate troops and cities were limited or non-existent. The troops were facing starvation. The Northern strategy of attrition had shattered the South.

Confederate General Robert E. Lee surrendered to Union General Ulysses S. Grant on April 9th, 1865, at the Appomattox Court House in Virginia. However, the war didn't end here. It took time for word of the surrender to spread, and in the meantime, small-scale battles continued. On April 26th, 1865, Florida surrendered.

War-weary Floridians reacted to the news differently. After realizing that the war would be ending soon, Florida's governor took his own life. Governor John Milton had stated that death would be more desirable to rejoining the United States. On April 1st, 1865, as the war was ebbing, Milton shot himself. Some today believe he died in a hunting accident, although research is still being conducted to verify this for certain.

When the Union troops arrived in Tallahassee, they unfurled and raised the flag of the United States. Occupation forces assumed control of the capital on May 10th, 1865. Leading the transition of power was Union Brigadier General Edward McCook. The Confederate troops surrendered. They also were required to sign papers agreeing not to fight and had to relinquish any military equipment.

The official ceremony transferring power to the federal government was held on May 20th, 1865. General McCook formally freed all enslaved Black people on that day. The Emancipation Proclamation was now law in Florida. Later that year, the United States ratified the Thirteenth Amendment, which outlawed slavery.

Residents of Florida faced an uncertain future. The impact of the war would be felt for generations. In addition to losing a third of the troops that Florida sent to fight in the war, another third returned physically injured. Others had invisible wounds that altered them and their families. Many veterans died within a few years after the war's end, demonstrating the incredible effects of the battles that had taken place.

The Southern states had been promised that they would be treated with respect and dignity by Ulysses S. Grant, the leader of the Union forces. However, the next steps for the country were determined by politicians.

With the North's victory in the Civil War, the issue of slavery was resolved. However, the resulting issues of reuniting the country and establishing the full rights of all citizens remained. Additionally, reprisals for those states seceding from the Union had not been decided, nor had the process of how and when to readmit the Southern states to the United States been clarified.

To rejoin the Union, the US government set stipulations. Florida initially refused to comply. In 1868, Florida accepted the terms of the Fourteenth Amendment to the US Constitution. The Fourteenth Amendment stipulated that all persons born in the US are citizens with equal protection under the law; thus, it gave citizenship to former slaves. On June 25th, 1868, Florida became a state again.

Chapter 7 – From Reconstruction to the 1920s Boom

Strife within states and between states intensified as a result of the Civil War. Rebuilding the country's infrastructure and political structure was a challenging time known as the Reconstruction era.

Once the war ended, soldiers returned home, many to small farms they had left behind. Freed slaves faced a time of uncertainty. They did not own land, nor did they have work or a place to live. Some freed slaves returned to the plantations where they had worked. However, plantation owners did not have money to pay for their labor.

Out of this dire situation emerged sharecropping. In this system, freed slaves paid to rent land from a plantation owner. Tenants, also known as sharecroppers, were required to give a percentage of their crops to their landlords, which was, for the most part, how they paid for the land. In addition, sharecroppers paid for goods and other expenses to local merchants and sometimes landlords. Ruthless landlords, high-interest rates, and unpredictable harvests kept most sharecroppers continually in debt.

While this system of tenant farming sustained some plantations during the transition from the war, it usually did not fully benefit the tenants. Most sharecroppers, who were frequently poorer Whites, although there was a good-sized number of freed slaves, could not fully pay off their debts. Oftentimes, Black sharecroppers worked for farmers or plantations where they had worked as slaves. Sharecropping or tenant farming continued for decades in Florida after the war.

Sharecropping perpetuated the oppression of African Americans in the South. Adding to the limitations placed on Black people was a set of restrictions called the Black Codes. Many Southern states, including Florida, passed these laws, which constrained the legal rights of Black people.

The former Confederate States used these laws as a means to reinstate the economic and constraining system of slavery, albeit without using that terminology. A stipulation in the Thirteenth Amendment prohibited slavery except as a punishment for crimes. The Black Codes criminalized seemingly minor infractions. For example, loitering and vagrancy were not permitted. Three or four Black people talking on a street corner could be considered loitering; therefore, a criminal act would have been committed.

Of all the Southern states who enacted Black Codes, Florida's were some of the most oppressive, and it rivaled Mississippi, which was perhaps the harshest state in regards to the codes. Some of Florida's former slave owners believed their rights to own enslaved people would return, thus justifying the subjugation of African Americans through the Black Codes. Charges of vagrancy in Florida could result in a one-year prison sentence. If a Black parent was sent to prison, any of their children could be hired as apprentices.

Florida was required to develop and pass a new state constitution for readmittance to the United States. President Andrew Johnson demanded that this constitution include Florida's repressive Black Codes being outlawed. The state had to pass the Fourteenth

Amendment as part of the rejoining process. This amendment states that all people born in the United States are citizens. Until this occurred, Johnson reestablished military rule in Florida.

On July 25th, 1868, Florida met President Johnson's conditions, and it was permitted to rejoin the United States. The writers of Florida's 1868 constitution were mainly members of the Republican Party. Their goal was to shape a future that would cause a dramatic change from the pre-war South. They sought to encourage and provide opportunities for newly freed slaves. Provisions in the constitution included access to public education, infrastructure improvements, and voting rights for all men.

Once Democrats started gaining control of local political offices, the ideals shaped by Florida's constitution began to disintegrate. By 1885, conservative Democrats dominated the legislature. That same year, a constitutional convention was called, and Florida rewrote its charter to reflect its current politics.

The delegates met in Tallahassee, where they decided to make significant changes. Florida had many government positions that were filled by political appointments. Now, many more political offices required elections. Florida's public schools would also be racially segregated. To lessen the perceived negative impact of voting rights for all men, Florida enacted poll taxes. This limited the voter base in the state, namely by eliminating, for the most part, the African American vote. Another significant provision was to outlaw marriages between White and Black people.

Since so few battles were fought in Florida, the people had not experienced the destruction of their land, which was fortunate for them. Other Southern states experienced such tremendous losses that their economies took years to recover.

The world was changing, and new industries were emerging. The 1880s started a time of tremendous development and the creation of new industries in Florida.

For instance, other states needed Florida's timber to rebuild. Expanding the Northern railway system into Florida would increase its access to trade with other states. However, Florida's debt from the Civil War limited its options to expand.

Northern investors viewed Florida as a land of opportunity. In 1881, Hamilton Disston, a wealthy business owner from the North, purchased four million acres of land in Florida. The land, which spanned from Orlando to Lake Okeechobee, which is the size of the state of Connecticut, was sold for twenty-five cents an acre.

Photograph of Hamilton Disston

Disston's investment allowed Florida to pay its debt from the Civil War. The vision he had was to alter Florida's water flow to create land that was more developable. The four million acres of land Disston purchased was swampy and continually filled with water. Immediately after his purchase, Disston began his project.

First, Lake Okeechobee was drained; its flow was diverted to the Caloosahatchee River, which sent it to the Gulf of Mexico. To control the water of the Kissimmee River, Disston had canals built. The new waterways rerouted Kissimmee's water to several different lakes. After completing these steps to re-engineer the flow of water, Disston was able to produce some farmable land. However, his results did not fully meet his lofty goals. A year after completing this phase of his project, it was noted that Florida had been in a drought. Disston's ideas did influence other developers and entrepreneurs who more successfully pursued similar ventures. In addition to the economic benefits of farming, controlling the swamps created a Florida that was more habitable. Around the vast farms that were developed, new towns arose from the former wetlands.

With a growing agricultural economy and the need for lumber, Florida now needed better access to the rest of the country. Another step in its transformation was building a railroad network. Henry B. Plant was the force behind Florida's rail system. In addition to the miles of track Plant laid in Florida, he connected Florida's train tracks to Georgia's railroads. This linked Florida to the rest of the country for the transportation of goods and people.

Photo of Henry B. Plant

Another industry spawned from the expansion of Florida's transportation system: the citrus industry. With the speed of the rails, food could be shipped from Florida to other states and still be fresh upon arrival. Citrus became a mainstay of Florida's economy.

Additionally, Plant erected hotels at important junctions in the railway system. The Tampa Bay Hotel is his best-known work. Constructed in 1891, the hotel cost almost three million dollars. Plant included modern amenities, such as electric lights. The hotel is now the location of the Henry B. Plant Museum.

Modern-day Henry B. Plant Museum

Complementing Plant's railroad work was William Chipley. He was also a builder of railways, and his tracks were laid in the Florida Panhandle. Placing railways in the Panhandle facilitated the transportation of supplies received at the ports of Pensacola. Supplies received at the seaport could then more readily be transported inland.

Advertisement for Flagler's East Coast Railway Streamliner

A third industrial and railway entrepreneur who made a tremendous impact on Florida was Henry M. Flagler. His wife's health necessitated a move to Florida. Flagler was extremely wealthy from his ownership of Standard Oil. When he first came to explore what Florida had to offer, he was disappointed with its accommodations and lack of an organized transportation system.

Flagler was captivated by the St. Augustine area, and he envisioned an American Riviera, a place where wealthy men from the North could visit in the winter. He built his first hotel. The opulent 540-room Ponce de Leon was completed in 1888. His next step was to create a network of railroads that could transport people to the area. Flagler purchased railroads and built any necessary connectors. His system of rail tracks linked St. Augustine and Daytona Beach to the North.

Continuing his vision of an American Riviera, Flagler went farther south to build a resort town for the wealthy. His next creation was Palm Beach. Coconut groves and oceanfront land provided an incredible vista for Flagler to begin his development. He created additional land by dredging a channel that transformed the swampy lands. To ensure his resort would have updated comforts, Flagler started a water and power system. His hotel, the Palm Beach Inn (later renamed The Breakers), was a beachfront luxury resort. His own home was a mansion named Whitehall, which was where he lived while in Palm Beach.

Whitehall today, which acts as a museum

Florida's warm, sunny weather was beginning to entice tourists to visit. Tourists who came reveled in Florida's beautiful beaches and landscapes. The improvements in transportation and lodging made Florida an accessible vacation destination, and the weather was also conducive to facilitating recovery from illnesses.

Besides the attention Florida was enjoying by the nation for its hospitality and goods, the situation in Cuba brought more interest. Cuba, which was a colony of Spain, is located ninety miles off the coast of Florida. Cubans began their war independence in 1895. Many in Florida supported the people of Cuba in their quest for freedom. The United States traded with Cuba and had businesses in Cuba. On top of that, there were US citizens who lived there.

In 1898, the United States declared war on Spain. The Spanish-American War began when the US warship, the *Maine*, sank in the harbor of Havana. No one knows if Spain caused the explosion (it was likely due to an internal problem), but the US accused them of sinking the ship. Newspapers around the country sensationalized the disaster, inflaming the people against the Spanish and prompting the US government to declare war. The explosion was merely the tipping point, as people had been itching to go to war before this point.

Florida ports were the launching points for United States troops being sent to Cuba. Miami and Tampa were used to establish training camps for troops. The fighting occurred mainly on Cuban soil, and the war lasted only a few months.

The Treaty of Paris ended the war. In the agreement, the US was given possession of Puerto Rico, the Philippines, and Guam as territories. Cuba was freed from Spain. Many of the soldiers and sailors, who were stationed or trained in Florida, remained in Florida. After the war was over, soldiers and sailors moved their families to join them in the Sunshine State.

Others joined the soldiers and sailors in their migration south to Florida. After the Spanish-American War, Florida saw a tremendous increase in its population. Many who moved were motivated by the year-long temperate climate. White New Englanders, who were escaping the cold and drawn by job prospects, caused Florida's White population to double by 1900. Freed slaves also migrated to Florida; they were motivated by the work opportunities in construction and on the railroads.

Immigration from other countries to Florida was also on the rise before the Spanish-American War, and it continued into the 1900s. With the unrest in Cuba, many Cubans sought a new life. Vincente Martinez Ybor was one such immigrant. Originally from Spain, he established a cigar company in Cuba. He later moved to Key West to avoid arrest, and he continued his work in the cigar business. Once Ybor's factory became successful, he needed skilled workers. Many emigrated from Cuba for economic opportunities and to escape Spanish rule.

Photograph of Vincente Martinez Ybor

Ybor City was founded in 1886, and it was known as the Cigar Capital of the World. Immigrants, mainly from Cuba, established a thriving city with opera houses, hotels, restaurants, and clubs. The upheaval of the Spanish-American War in Cuba prompted more Cubans to seek refuge in Ybor City.

Turmoil in Greece, which was due to hundreds of years of Ottoman rule, set off a wave of emigration from Greece to Florida. In the early 1900s, Greeks faced an uncertain future in their country. Greece had been damaged from years of war, and the people had few possibilities of meaningful work. Immigrants relocated to Tarpon Springs, Florida.

Located on the Gulf of Mexico, Tarpon Springs offered job opportunities that mirrored the immigrants' previous existence on islands in the Aegean Sea. Sponge diving and the fishing industry created a Greek enclave in Tarpon Springs. John Cheyney is believed to have started the sponge industry there in 1905, and it eventually became known as the Sponge Capital of the World. Tarpon Springs still holds that title, with around 95 percent of sea sponges coming from the city. Greek traditions, restaurants, and industries flourished in Tarpon Springs.

A sponge harvest from the early 2000s

Though Florida had experienced an influx of immigrants, it still had an abundance of uninhabited flat land. And with Florida's temperate climate, the state was a choice location for US military operations during World War I. Florida's participation in the war included providing land for training bases and increasing food production. Additionally, over forty-two thousand Floridians served in the armed forces of the United States. Thirty percent of the troops from Florida were African Americans.

Throughout the United States' involvement in WWI, Florida supplied a significant percentage of citrus crops to troops overseas. Similar to other states, residents of Florida contributed to the war effort by reducing their consumption of food and other materials needed for the war.

The Pensacola Naval Station was established in 1913. Many firsts were documented at the innovative station. Some of the first established altitude records and catapult launches from a ship took place here. It was also, unfortunately, the home of the first fatal US Navy air crash.

Simultaneously, non-military air travel was expanding, with many record-setting events occurring in Florida. In 1914, the first routinely scheduled commercial flight path was established. Though this route was short-lived, it demonstrated the power of air travel. The St. Petersburg-Tampa Airboat flight took only twenty-three minutes. That was eleven hours less than rail travel between the two cities.

The country was becoming increasingly connected by travel. World War I also began changing the type of work available in the North. More factory jobs were created to meet the demands of the war. Many of these jobs continued after the war ended.

Opportunities were greater for African Americans in the North than in the South. Referred to as the Great Migration, more than 400,000 Black people left the fields of the South. Florida experienced an exodus of tens of thousands of African Americans in the years between 1915 and 1918. This massive departure for Northern cities changed the demographics of the country.

Another outcome of World War I was an increase in Americans' discretionary income. Along with the pay differences between factory work and farm work were the benefits. More workers were receiving paid vacation time and retirement incomes. For Florida, this meant more tourists, new residents, and owners of second homes.

Land was bought and sold sight-unseen. Prices for land skyrocketed. Purchasing on credit was a new phenomenon. The ability to purchase land on credit increased the number of investors in Florida's land boom. Investors sought to buy low and sell high. The Florida legislature passed laws to encourage land speculation. People were making a lot of money until the land boom went bust.

Chapter 8 – The Great Depression and WWII

Florida's economic highs of the 1920s began to fall toward the middle of the decade. The days of land purchases occurring without seeing the land had negative ramifications. Acres of swampland were sold as part of the buying frenzy, and draining the land was costly, leading to deals collapsing.

Many land purchases were completed with a binder on the deal. Binders are non-refundable down payments on a piece of land. Someone buying land using a binder was expected to pay the balance of the sale price within thirty days. Many of these buyers were land speculators who gambled that the value of their purchase would increase in the thirty days before the balance was due. As a result of this, some did not have the money to pay the balance that was due.

With the land boom, prices skyrocketed. Rent and housing prices did as well. Florida was no longer the affordable location it had been touted to be. Residents and newspapers recommend to those people thinking about relocating not to move to Florida.

The seemingly endless flow of money and credit ceased. Banks and investors no longer believed in "paper millionaires," so money lending was halted. Land values plunged to record lows, and property foreclosures began.

Weather added to the complicated scene. People moved to Florida for the great weather. However, when the winter of 1925 arrived, it was extremely cold. The summer of 1926 was exceptionally hot. This caused Florida's reputation of being a weather paradise to be called into question.

Further damage to Florida's "Sunshine State" moniker occurred in 1926 and 1928. Two crippling hurricanes caused considerable damage. Flooding and high winds caused significant property damage. The hurricane of 1928 struck the Palm Beach area. Winds of over 130 miles per hour wreaked havoc. Lake Okeechobee flooded, and over two thousand people drowned. Over fifty thousand people were left homeless. It remains one of the deadliest hurricanes in the United States.

The aftermath of the hurricane in Palm Beach

Nature was not done with Florida. To wrap up the 1920s, the Mediterranean fruit fly attacked the citrus crops. Fruit flies rapidly infested grapefruit and orange groves across the state, decimating about 60 percent of the crops. The remaining crops were quarantined. Roadblocks were established to search for anyone leaving the state with citrus fruit.

Florida was in the unenviable position of having had a four-year head start on the Great Depression. The stock market crash of 1929 leveled the economy of the whole country. Stocks lost their value, which means investors lost everything. Businesses closed, people lost their jobs, and banks foreclosed on homes.

There were no easy remedies for the devastating collapse of the country's or even Florida's economy. The state legislature in Florida tried legalized betting as a means to boost tax revenues. The State Racing Commission was formed in 1931. Horse and dog races were open for wagering. In addition, gambling on results of jai alai games was legal. The commission had taxes taken from the winner's purse. However, the people did not have any money to wager bets. Thus, unfortunately, legalized betting did not end the depression in Florida.

By 1932, numerous banks had shuttered their doors. Once the banks were closed, people did not have access to their money and lost their savings. Without work and without savings, families could not afford to pay their rents or mortgages, nor could people pay to eat or buy goods. This had a domino effect leading to more closed businesses. One-quarter of all Floridians lived on government aid.

Tourism, which was once a key element of Florida's winter economy, struggled. Some tourists still drove south to escape the winter cold and dreariness of the North. However, the Florida State Police were positioned on Florida's border. The tourists that were trying to enter the state needed to prove that they had enough money to support themselves. If they did not, they were denied entrance into the state. Florida could not afford to support more people.

In the presidential election of 1932, Franklin D. Roosevelt ran against the incumbent President Hoover. The country, weary from the Great Depression, sought a change. Floridians supported Roosevelt, who won in a landslide.

Franklin D. Roosevelt took the oath of office as president of the United States in 1933. When campaigning for the presidency, Roosevelt promised Americans that he had solutions to the Great Depression. His program was dubbed the New Deal. The New Deal, also nicknamed Alphabet Soup, created several agencies that were tasked with returning people to work under federal programs. President Roosevelt also suggested labor reforms, including a minimum wage and working conditions.

Though everyone could agree that farms needed assistance to survive and that people needed jobs, Floridians were concerned about the overreach of the federal government. Business leaders and conservatives were leery of Roosevelt's sweeping reforms. Due to these suspicions, local politicians pursued methods to obtain federal money without federal bureaucracy.

Roosevelt's administration was politically savvy, though. His officials positioned Florida leaders on key committees to garner support. Floridians remained cautious about the federal government controlling Florida banks and other establishments. Publicly, however, most politicians supported the New Deal.

During the same election cycle, in 1932, Floridians elected a new governor named David Sholtz, an acquaintance of the newly elected president. Although he was a transplanted New Yorker, he won the election. He highlighted a return to Florida's fundamental industries as a solution to its current economic woes.

With his Northern connections, Sholtz embraced many aspects of Roosevelt's New Deal. His administration established many of the local agencies needed to connect with the federal government. Sholtz created the State Welfare Board, the State Planning Board, and the Emergency Relief Administration. Florida was poised to accept federal aid.

A photo of Sholtz (middle) and FDR (left)

One new agency formed as a component of the New Deal was the Civilian Conservation Corps, also known simply as the CCC. In Florida, over fifty thousand young men worked as part of the CCC. A six-month commitment was required to participate. Those selected to serve in the program lived in work camps, where they were provided food and clothing. In return, these men sent home their paychecks to their families. Workers earned thirty dollars each month; of that money, twenty-five dollars a month had to be sent home.

Eight new parks were developed by the CCC in Florida. Landscape designers toiled alongside CCC workers to design parks that complemented Florida's natural environment. Structures were built with native building resources. In addition, the CCC planted thirteen million trees throughout Florida.

The Overseas Railroad, which was constructed by Henry Flagler and connected Miami to Key West, was destroyed by a hurricane. The CCC rebuilt the one-hundred-mile-long railroad. Forty bridges were included in the restoration project. When tourists started returning to Florida, the railroad became an important means of transportation.

Other construction projects were accomplished under the Public Works Administration, also known as the PWA. Some of the jobs they worked on were a continuation of projects started when Florida experienced its land boom. Once the land boom ceased, projects immediately stopped, regardless of the progress. One key construction project that the PWA completed was installing a dike around Lake Okeechobee. The dike was supposed to control water flow during hurricanes.

Another legacy from the New Deal projects was the WPA or Works Progress Administration. Under this agency, work was created for authors, researchers, teachers, and historians. Zora Neale Hurston, who was born in Alabama but spent most of her life in Florida, detailed the life history of people who had been slaves and immigrants. She captured their stories and cultural backgrounds. After her work for the WPA, she became a well-known author. Her best-known work is her novel *Their Eyes Were Watching God.*

Photo of Zora Neale Hurston

Positive effects resulted from many of the New Deal programs. Businesses in Florida began to rebound. One of the men propelling Florida's banking industry toward recovery was Alfred du Pont. His family made their fortune in gunpowder, and he used that wealth to buy banks in Florida. Du Pont u infused new capital into the banks, restoring part of Florida's banking industry. In addition, du Pont purchased 300,000 acres of forests. Then he purchased the St. Joe Paper Company and revitalized the company and the town in which it was located.

Photograph of Alfred du Pont

By the close of the decade, the United States was emerging from the Great Depression. Florida's tourism industry was prospering. The rebuilt roads, railroads, and a growing airline industry increased the nation's access to Florida as a vacation destination.

On the heels of the Great Depression came another cataclysmic event that once again affected the whole world. This was none other than World War II, which lasted from 1939 to 1945. The war, as terrible as it was, brought the world out of the Great Depression. Florida's weather and flat terrain made it a key player in the war for the United States.

Due to the size of Florida and its relatively lightly populated areas, it was ideal for military training bases. The Army Air Corps operated from Drew and MacDill Airfields in Tampa, Eglin at Fort Walton Beach, Dale Mabry in Tallahassee, and Orlando Field. The US Army also reestablished Carlstrom Field, which was located in Arcadia, for flight training.

The US Navy utilized the Pensacola Naval Station, which allowed them to increase their presence. They also created a naval air station, which is now home to the famous Blue Angels (a flight demonstration squadron established in 1946). The US Navy also added locations, such as Banana River in Eau Gallie, Cecil Field and Mayport in Jacksonville, Camp Blanding in Starke, and the Key West Naval Station. Not only did American pilots train in Florida, but the British Royal Force also had locations in Arcadia and the University of Miami.

Florida's network of flight training stations was so extensive that the majority of US pilots during WWII had a connection to one or more of Florida's air bases. At the start of the war, Florida had 172 total military locations. Days after the attack on Pearl Harbor and the US entry into the war in late 1941, Pensacola ramped up its training accommodations by 300 percent. Pilots who were trained at the Pensacola Naval Air Station accounted for the sinking of over sixty German submarines. In addition, these Navy and Marine aviators downed over 15,000 Japanese planes while losing 451 US planes to Japan. The group trained in Pensacola also accounted for the destruction of 161 Japanese warships.

Camp Blanding was another key location for the US military during WWII. It was initially constructed as one of the New Deal projects through the WPA, and it was built on twenty-eight thousand acres. During the war, its size increased to 180,000 acres, with much of this land being obtained through eminent domain and leases from local landowners. During the height of the war effort, Camp Blanding grew into Florida's fourth-largest city. Over 745,000 personnel were trained there.

The dramatic surge in training needs and personnel overwhelmed the existing on-base accommodations. More facilities were needed, and the military's solution was to assume control of hotels near the training bases. Hundreds of motels and hotels were utilized by the United States military for barracks. Some facilities were needed for personnel who returned home injured from the conflict, which means hotels and motels had to be repurposed as hospitals. Some of the more well-known facilities that were appropriated were the Don CeSar in St. Petersburg, The Breakers and the Hollywood Beach Hotel in Fort Lauderdale, and the Biltmore Hotel in Coral Gables.

While battles were not fought on US soil, the Germans and their warcraft did enter America's coastal waters. Early in the war, the United States Navy was woefully unprepared to counter the Axis Powers of Germany, Japan, and Italy. The Axis alliance had superior capability in regard to planes and warships.

German U-boats, which were sophisticated submarines, successfully sank over thirty-five ships located along Florida's coast. On April 10th, 1942, German *U-123* destroyed the US tanker SS *Gulfamerica*. The tanker was returning from Texas filled with oil, a precious wartime product, when it was attacked. Its explosive cargo created a spectacular fire off the coast of Jacksonville Beach. The U-boat surfaced and fired at the tanker. Nineteen members of *Gulfamerica*'s crew perished in the attack. Florida's Governor Spessard Holland, who was governor for much of the war, instituted blackout orders along the coast in response.

As the US Navy and Coast Guard grew their fleets, they were able to escort ships along America's coast. Also assisting in the effort to protect Florida's coastline was the Civil Air Patrol (CAP). The CAP's civilian force effectively supported the military in protecting Florida's coast. Thousands of volunteers assisted, and the trained spotters monitored flights and other air action along the shoreline.

Despite the increased safeguards, German spies did come ashore near Ponte Vedra Beach. In June 1942, four agents accessed Florida's coast on *U-584.* Once ashore, they hid explosives in the dunes on Ponte Vedra Beach along with other equipment needed for future missions. This group traveled north to New York and Chicago to meet with other saboteurs. They were tasked with bombing important US railroads, bridges, and factories. One member of the New York group turned himself in to the FBI. All were tried, and the four who came ashore in Florida were executed.

World War II ended in 1945. Millions died worldwide as a result of the war and the atrocities committed by the Nazis in Germany. Throughout the war effort, people made sacrifices to ensure there would be enough materials for wartime production.

WWII generated unprecedented growth in the economy. The Great Depression was officially over. Unemployment was no longer a major concern. Contracts rebuilt Florida's businesses and established many new industries. On top of this, the jobs created during the war paid well. This created a resurgence of tourism in Florida.

Before WWII, most jobs in manufacturing and farming were held by men throughout the country. Once the United States actively sent troops to support the Allied forces, women were needed in the workplace to replace the men who left. While single women worked in traditional women's roles, to keep up with wartime production, married women had to join the efforts, even though they would have traditionally stayed home with their children.

In Florida, Southern Dairy now had milkmaids instead of milkmen. Florida Power & Light hired women as pole painters. Planting, plowing, and harvesting were done on Florida farms by women during the war. Shipyards in Pensacola, Panama City, Tampa, and Jacksonville relied on women.

Through the efforts of Florida's Mary McLeod Bethune, the US Army opened a training location in Daytona Beach. Mary McLeod Bethune, who was from Palatka, Florida, was the founder of the

National Council of Negro Women. Through her work, she became involved at the national level as President Franklin Delano Roosevelt's only female on his Black Cabinet.

When WWII began, tourism in Florida halted. The leaders of Daytona Beach were concerned about their economy and called upon McLeod Bethune for assistance. She was able to convince FDR to create a training facility in Daytona Beach for the Women's Auxiliary Army Corps, or WAAC. Over twenty thousand women trained for WAAC in Florida.

The face of American workers evolved during the war years. With so many men serving in the military, women had to work in the public sector on a larger scale. Women proved they were capable of filling the roles previously dominated by men. After the war and once White male veterans returned, the face of the American worker returned to its prewar image.

Chapter 9 – Civil Rights Movement and the Cold War

Soldiers and sailors returned home to Florida at the conclusion of World War II, and they were greeted with a strong economy. New industries and jobs had melded with Florida's cornerstone enterprises of citrus, cattle, phosphate, and tourism. The newly constructed interstate highway system provided mobility for Floridians and visitors. The end of the 1940s saw much optimism.

During the war, Florida eclipsed California as the top producer of citrus. Florida citrus growers created and patented the process to produce frozen concentrated orange juice. Other agricultural industries were also expanding and becoming more profitable. In 1945, dichlorodiphenyltrichloroethane (better known as DDT) became available for public sale. It was thought that DDT would aid in the development of farming, as it was a powerful insecticide. DDT was one of the first modern synthetic insecticides, and it was formulated in a US Department of Agricultural lab in Orlando. Its long-term effects were not known at the time, although there was some early vocal opposition against it. It is now widely known that DDT causes environmental damage. In 1972, it was banned in the United

States for agricultural use. Due to this ban, the population numbers of both the bald eagle and the peregrine falcon have increased.

Another change to Florida post-WWII was the expansion of air conditioning. Due to the proliferation of air conditioning, the tourism industry expanded. Florida was now accessible to visitors during the hot summer months. Air-conditioned automobiles and railcars allowed people to travel to Florida in greater comfort, again increasing the volume of tourists.

Air conditioning started a shift in Florida society. Before air conditioning, people sat on their front porches to keep cool. Neighbors could easily socialize with each other as a result. Modern air conditioning kept more people indoors. Additionally, Florida began to transition from a rural agrarian society to one based more on manufacturing and urban settings.

Along with the shift to move to cities was the population swell. During the war effort, people moved to Florida for jobs and military training. Towns and cities more than doubled in size. Tens of thousands of people migrated to Florida during the 1940s, and many of them stayed. Its population increased by over 40 percent.

Another transformation that was a result of the war (although it had been centuries in the making) was the fight for equality. Hitler's genocide against the Jewish people was a terrible atrocity. Since the United States was willing to battle Hitler and what he stood for, African Americans throughout the country began to hope for actual change. The Florida chapter of the NAACP (the National Association for the Advancement of Colored People) began a campaign dubbed the "Double V." The "V" stood for victory. The NAACP was campaigning for victory against racism in Germany and in the United States. Segregation in the South was still prevalent even though it was nearly a century after the end of the Civil War. World War II and its aftermath were the fuel for the Civil Rights movement.

The end of the Civil War and the ratification of the Thirteenth Amendment, which abolished slavery, did not bring about the equality that had been envisioned by President Abraham Lincoln's Emancipation Proclamation. On the one-hundredth anniversary of Lincoln's birth in 1909, the NAACP was formed. A series of meetings were held to address concerns over the recent race riots in Illinois and the high number of lynchings. This interracial committee created an organization that would work toward political, educational, social, and economic equality.

After the Civil War and throughout the period of the Reconstruction, laws were passed, mainly in the South, to thwart the assimilation of newly freed slaves into society. The Black Codes, also known as the Jim Crow laws, legalized segregation. Severe consequences, which sometimes even included death, were applied to anyone who broke these laws.

Simultaneous to the establishment of the Black Codes (at least those passed after the Civil War) was the formation of the Ku Klux Klan or the KKK. The KKK started as a private club for disenfranchised Civil War veterans, and it grew to symbolize and enact a warped vigilante justice. Known for covering themselves in white hoods, KKK members terrorized and targeted Blacks, Jews, Catholics, and others. One of the key reasons the NAACP was formed was to address and eliminate lynchings from KKK members.

In Florida, membership in the NAACP flourished during and after World War II. The workforce had to become more diverse to meet the wartime demands of production. Members of the NAACP were able to find support for their grievances against racial barriers in the military and workforce. Changes were starting to happen.

Harry T. Moore was an active member of the NAACP. In 1934, he formed the first branch of the NAACP in Brevard County (located on the eastern coast of Florida). Throughout his tenure working with the NAACP, Moore organized fifty additional chapters of the organization. While Black people could not run for office at this time,

Moore knew that if he encouraged enough Black people to vote, change would occur. Moore is credited with registering more than 100,000 new Black voters.

Prior to Moore's actions, many disincentives were applied to keep Black voters away from the voting booths. Strict residency requirements, literacy tests, poll taxes, and intimidation of Black voters reduced the percentage of Black people who voted. For instance, the KKK would drive through Black neighborhoods with nooses. By threatening African Americans in this manner, the KKK ensured that Blacks had no voice at the polls. In 1940, only 3 percent of Black people in the South of voting age were registered to vote.

Photograph of Harry T. Moore

Moore fought for and won equal pay for Black teachers in Florida. His activism extended to investigating lynchings of Black people that were happening in Florida. Moore and his wife were both fired from their jobs as teachers due to their crusading efforts for change.

In 1949, Moore became involved in the Groveland Four case. Four young Black men were accused of raping a White woman. One of the young men, Ernest Thomas, was killed by a large posse before the case reached the courts. He was shot an astounding four hundred times. The three remaining defendants were convicted by an all-White jury. Moore sought to have the conviction reversed due to the lack of evidence. His work took the case to the Florida Supreme Court.

In 1951, the case against Shepherd and Irvin was heard by the United States Supreme Court. The two were defended by NAACP attorney Thurgood Marshall. The court's decision to overturn the conviction was unanimous. Marshall won a new trial for Shepherd and Irvin.

A local law enforcement officer, Sheriff Willis McCall, transported two of the young men (Samuel Shepherd and Walter Irvin) back to the local jail. Though they were handcuffed, McCall claimed that they attacked him. McCall shot each of them three times. He killed Shepherd and wounded Irvin. Charles Greenlee, the fourth young man, was not in the sheriff's custody at the time.

Harry Moore demanded that criminal charges be filed against the sheriff. He also called on Florida's governor to remove McCall from office while the charges were being investigated. Six weeks later, on December 25th, 1951, the Moore's house was bombed. Both Harry and Harriette Moore died as a result of the attack on their house. They were the first martyrs of the civil rights movement.

In November 2021, the Groveland Four were all exonerated.

The landscape of Florida's educational system began to change in 1950. Oliver Brown, who at the time was just a welder, was recruited by the NAACP to take part in the lawsuit to desegregate schools. The lawsuit would ultimately be filed under his name. By 1954, the case had reached the US Supreme Court. A unanimous ruling in *Brown v. Board of Education of Topeka* said that separate but equal schools were unconstitutional.

Emboldened by support from the Supreme Court, student groups and local leaders planned protests to effect changes to other discriminatory practices. Two students from Florida Agricultural and Mechanical University (Florida A&M), Carrie Patterson and Wilhelmina Jakes, sat in the Whites-only section of a bus. At this time, the front of the bus was reserved for White people, while Black people had to sit in the back. When these young ladies refused to give up their seats, they were arrested. The Tallahassee bus boycott began. Black residents refused to ride buses for seven months. In December of 1956, the US Supreme Court ruled that segregation on public buses violated the constitution.

In the early 1960s, the Tallahassee Congress of Racial Equality (CORE) planned two sit-ins at Woolworth, a department store. Students from Florida A&M University sat in the Whites-only section of the lunch counter. They were arrested for their refusal to leave, and eleven of the students were charged with disturbing the peace. They had the option to pay a fine or spend sixty days in jail. Eight of the eleven opted for jail time. The Tallahassee jail-in was the first of the civil rights movement.

After the students had served their jail time, former First Lady Eleanor Roosevelt assisted the CORE group in raising funds for their activities. Other groups of students continued to advocate for desegregation. The Tallahassee Ten fought for the right to eat at a segregated airport restaurant. More students protested segregation at the State Theatre in Tallahassee. Over four hundred students were arrested, causing the creation of an overflow jail at the Leon County Fairgrounds.

Dr. Martin Luther King Jr. joined Florida's protesters in 1964. As he walked up to the Monson Motor Lodge's restaurant in St. Augustine, he was arrested. Black and White activists planned to stage a wade-in at the motel's pool. The motel's owner doused the group in the pool with acid. Newspapers worldwide printed pictures of the horrifying scene.

The infamous picture of the hotel manager pouring acid into the pool

During the summer of 1964, US Congress was considering civil rights legislation. Scenes from the wade-in in St. Augustine helped sway lawmakers in their vote. On July 2nd, 1964, President Lyndon B. Johnson signed the Civil Rights Act. The law now prohibited employment discrimination, mandated equal access to public locations, and upheld the desegregation of schools and the right to vote.

Around the same time that this transformation of discriminatory social practices was occurring in the United States, Cuba was going through a revolution. In 1959, Fidel Castro's communist regime ousted the military dictatorship of Fulgencio Batista. Supporters of the Batista government sought refuge in Florida, particularly around the Miami area. This group was followed by many affluent Cubans, who had their wealth seized by Castro's government. This first wave of Cuban immigrants believed they would return home after their country was liberated.

Batista, though a dictator, had been against communism, and he supported the United States and its economic interests in the island. Once Castro assumed power, the US sought ways to remove him from power. These actions culminated with the Bay of Pigs invasion in 1961. Some of the training for the Bay of Pigs invasion occurred on Useppa Island, which is off Florida's coast near Fort Meyers. Useppa Island was the first covert base that the Central Intelligence Agency (CIA) operated from in Florida. Many recruits for the mission were newly arrived Cuban immigrants currently living in Miami.

The United States felt it had the support of many people remaining in Cuba and the Cuban refugees to oust Castro. The failed invasion lasted less than one day and left Castro securely in power. Actually, the failed invasion solidified Castro's power instead of removing him from office. Castro's popularity increased in Cuba, and the failed operation fueled the anti-American climate there.

This meant the new residents of Florida had to start their new lives in a new country. When they fled Cuba, they had left everything behind. Former mill owners now accepted jobs as custodians. Thousands in the Miami area have family success stories about rebuilding their lives.

Castro's political repression and the country's economic difficulties culminated in a second wave of immigration to the United States. Due to the closure of thousands of small businesses, former supporters of Castro began to disavow the revolution. In part to eliminate the dissenters, Castro opened Cuba's borders to let people leave. Thousands of refugees tried to cross the waters from Cuba to Florida.

The sheer number of people overwhelmed both countries, greatly affecting population demographics.

The United States and Cuba agreed to help process the flow of people through Freedom Flights, which lasted from 1965 to 1973. Planes would fly from Cuba to Miami five days a week, often doing two runs in a single day. Over 300,000 people partook in the opportunity to flee Castro's oppressive regime. Miami became home to thousands of new arrivals. Within Miami, Little Havana was a welcoming location for displaced Cubans.

The third wave of Cuban immigrants to Florida occurred in 1980. Referred to as the Mariel Boatlift, Castro opened his borders to those seeking to leave. Over 125,000 Cubans emigrated from their country. This wave of immigrants saw many from the working class who had once supported Castro. Castro also forcefully deported criminals, those from the LGBT community, prostitutes, and people who had been admitted into mental hospitals.

Historically, Cuba and the United States have been allies. After Castro's takeover of Cuba, anti-communist refugees were welcomed in the United States. In 1966, the Cuban Adjustment Act was passed. This law paved a smoother and quicker path to citizenship for Cuban immigrants who met certain criteria.

Of all the people who emigrated from Cuba, 60 percent live in Florida. Miami's population of Cubans was around fifty thousand in 1960. By 1980, there were more than 580,000 Cubans living in the Miami area. The initial groups of immigrants founded businesses and made the transition for subsequent groups easier. The Florida Cuban Heritage Trail highlights the path of Cuban immigration. The Calle Ocho Festival is the largest Latin music festival in the US, and it is celebrated in Miami in March.

The issues with Cuba during the 1960s stem from the Cold War, which was just one of the results of the end of World War II. The Cold War came about partly due to the United States asserting its nuclear dominance by dropping the atomic bomb on Japan and

Russia's gradual takeover of countries in Eastern Europe. Though shots were never fired, this war lasted from 1945 to 1991, and it impacted almost every country in the world.

With Cuba just ninety miles from Florida, the impact of Castro's developing relationship with the Soviet Union was a cause for great concern. The Soviet Union provided support for Castro during his successful revolution and assumption of power. One result of the United States' attempt to invade Cuba was a strengthening of the relationship between Cuba and the Soviet Union. When Castro requested support from the Soviet Union, Russia supplied Cuba with nuclear weapons. Castro declared Cuba a socialist state that was aligned with the Eastern Bloc countries.

The placement of nuclear weapons only ninety miles from Florida frightened Americans. During October and November 1962, for thirteen tense days, the United States and the Soviet Union faced off in the Cuban Missile Crisis. A successful resolution to the confrontation was found, which resulted in the removal of nuclear armaments from Cuba.

Shortly after the resolution of the Cuban Missile Crisis, the US Army Corps of Engineers constructed the Nike Hercules missile site. Its location in the Everglades was a defensive posture, with the intention of protecting the United States from any missile attacks from the south. About 140 soldiers staffed this site while it was operational; it ceased operations in 1979. When the facilities were completed in 1965, the site housed three missile barns, a missile assembly building, Nike Hercules missiles, and other support structures. The site is now listed on the US Department of the National Register of Historic Places.

Florida's location made it desirable for the US Air Force to develop its missile program. The favorable climate in Florida provided opportunities for year-round launches. Cold War hostilities between the United States and the Soviet Union propelled the development of the National Aeronautics and Space Administration, or NASA, in 1958. This was a civilian branch of the government, and it would take over the management of the exploration of space. It replaced NACA, the National Advisory Committee for Aeronautics. NASA was designed to seek more peacetime applications for space exploration.

In addition to the building of nuclear weapons by both countries, the two world powers were engaged in a space race. Both countries sought to validate their dominance over the other. The US and the USSR sought to claim new territory in space and prove their technological superiority. Leaders of these two countries felt as if space was literally their next frontier. Florida became a key location for the United States in its attempt to win the space race. In 1949, missile testing was launched from Cape Canaveral; this was the first step in creating Florida's Space Coast.

After successfully launching Sputnik in 1957, the Soviets took a significant lead in the Space Race, which was an extension of the Cold War. Sputnik 1 was the first manmade craft that entered Earth's orbit. This was followed the next year by Sputnik II. In 1961, Yuri Gagarin became the first person in the world to go into space; he represented the Soviet Union. The world, especially the US, was shocked. The Russians had been decimated as a result of World War II; however, they beat the United States in the space race.

Florida benefited greatly from the space race with the development of the Space Coast. Brevard County and Cape Canaveral grew exponentially in response to the Soviets' success. Explorer I was launched from Cape Canaveral in 1958, becoming the first US satellite to be sent to space.

President John F. Kennedy issued NASA its next significant challenge in a speech in 1961, which is frequently referred to as his "Moon Speech." He declared that the United States would put a man on the moon before the end of the decade: "We choose to go to the moon...in this decade and do the other things, not because they are easy, but because they are hard." Fear that the Soviets could now launch nuclear warheads from Sputnik propelled the United States into action.

With Kennedy's support, NASA's budget increased dramatically. Its budget in 1961 was $744 million. This was a 500 percent increase in spending, and it provided NASA with a $2,552 million dollar budget in 1964.

To prepare for this mission, NASA obtained over ninety thousand acres of land on Merritt Island. Project Mercury was a series of crewed space flights that launched from Cape Canaveral. Alan Shepard piloted the first manned space mission in 1961; the next year, John Glenn became the first US astronaut to orbit Earth. In 1963, President Kennedy was assassinated, and Cape Canaveral was renamed Cape Kennedy, although it returned to its original name ten years later. The NASA Launch Operations Center was also renamed, becoming the Kennedy Space Center, and that name stuck. Kennedy had just visited the space center six days before his death.

Kennedy's vision of a lunar landing continued to be pursued. Building upon the knowledge gained with Project Mercury, NASA established the Gemini Program. Two astronauts were launched into space in larger vessels from the Kennedy Space Center. Ten manned and two unmanned missions were flown as part of Gemini.

The Apollo program was designed for crewed missions to the moon with lunar landings. Its first mission was scheduled to launch from Cape Canaveral in February 1967. A pre-launch test of the spacecraft on January 27th, 1967, resulted in a fatal fire. All three crew members—Gus Grissom, Edward H. White, and Roger B. Chaffee—were killed in a fire on Launch Pad 34 in Cape Canaveral. The speed at which the space program was progressing made it a risky endeavor for all the countries involved. An investigation into the cause of the fire and then a reworking of the Apollo space modules to prevent other catastrophes resulted in a one-year postponement of other missions.

The Apollo Program brought to fruition Kennedy's vision of a man on the moon. On July 16th, 1969, Apollo II successfully launched from the Kennedy Space Center in Florida. Neil Armstrong, Buzz Aldrin, and Michael Collins piloted the spacecraft. Armstrong's historic moonwalk occurred on July 20th, with people from around the world tuning in to see. The Space Race was officially over, and the United States had emerged as the triumphant winner.

A photograph taken of Buzz Aldrin

Another marvel of dreams and visions was occurring to the west of Brevard County. Disneyland had opened in California in 1955. Florida's available undeveloped land and highway system made it Walt Disney's next enterprise. In the Orlando area, significant tracts of undeveloped swampland were purchased by a number of small companies. Real estate agents were not aware who was purchasing the land until Walt Disney had the acreage he required. He dubbed the purchase the "Florida Project."

He had learned from his experiences building Disneyland in California, as that theme park had quickly become landlocked. Walt Disney was attracted to Florida because of its weather, interstate road system, and the amount of open land that he could purchase. He wanted to create a theme park, not just an amusement park. As part of the experience, Disney wanted multiple venues within the complex. He wanted this to be a destination, not just a side attraction that people would visit on their trips.

Construction on Walt Disney's dream commenced in the 1960s. Walt died from cancer in 1966 before the construction of Disney World even began. His brother, Roy, came out of retirement and assumed leadership of the project. The first part of Disney World, Magic Kingdom, greeted visitors in 1971.

A photograph taken of Cinderella's Castle at Walt Disney World

In 1982, EPCOT, which is an acronym for Experimental Prototype Community of Tomorrow, was the second of the parks. This was followed by Hollywood Studios (originally named Disney-MGM Studios) and Animal Kingdom. In addition, Disney World has two waterparks, over two dozen hotels, golf courses, entertainment venues, and shops on its over thirty thousand acres.

The creation of Disney World changed theme parks and Florida itself. Leaders of the state and local governments worked closely and cooperatively with Disney's representatives. This relationship added to the success of Disney's venture. Disney and Florida are terms often used synonymously. Tourism is a key component of Florida's economy, and visitors to Disney are a significant element of that part of Florida's revenue base.

Chapter 10 – The Hurricanes of Nature and Politics

In the 1980s and 1990s, after the fall of the Soviet Union, governments in Central and South America, as well as the Caribbean, faced uncertainty. Instability in this region led to another wave of new residents in Florida. Many were escaping from countries that were facing inflation, unemployment, and political unrest. The new arrivals built upon the communities developed by Cuban immigrants.

Immigrants became established members of Florida's society. Bob Martinez was born in Tampa to Spanish immigrants. He eventually became the mayor of the city, serving from 1979 to 1986. Some of his accomplishments as mayor include one of the first trash-to-energy plants in the US, building a performing arts center, and the restoration of the 1915 City Hall building.

Building upon his successes in Tampa, Bob Martinez was successful in his bid to become Florida's first governor of Spanish descent in 1986. Governor Martinez increased funding to purchase land for conservation efforts. Three billion dollars' worth of land was bought under Preservation 2000, which was the largest land acquisition program in the country. Other acts that Martinez proposed protected water, manatees, and dolphins.

In 1991, Martinez was appointed the nation's drug czar by President George H. Bush. Although he ended up leaving his career in politics, he remained heavily involved in non-profit work. In 2009, he was honored as part of the Great Floridians Program.

Florida is known for its sunshine and warm weather due to its location. However, that same location makes it prone to hurricanes. Located near the tropics and in the path of the westerly winds that blow off the coast of Africa, Florida frequently ends up experiencing the effects of hurricanes.

It is believed that the word "hurricane" comes from the Taíno word *juracán,* which means "evil spirit of the wind." The root of the word is from the Maya god for bad weather. Spanish explorers in the Florida area probably learned the word from the Taíno.

Hurricane Andrew dealt a blow to southern Florida in 1992. This was the first major storm to pummel Florida in twenty-five years, and it caused over twenty-five billion dollars in damages. Sixty-three thousand homes were demolished. Over eighty-two thousand businesses in Andrew's path of annihilation were destroyed. This highlighted the need to change building codes in Florida in preparation for future hurricanes.

A mobile park after the hurricane swept through

A few years later, Florida suffered a relentless hurricane season. In the 2004-2005 season, the state was struck by seven major hurricanes. Florida was renamed the "Plywood State" by the media because many buildings were boarded up for a long period of time. Every part of Florida felt the impact of these storm events.

In 2004, one storm after another battered Florida. Within a six-week period, five storms made impactful landfall. Some of the same areas were continually battered. Clean-up and rebuilding efforts were almost impossible. Flooding, power outages, closed roads, and contaminated water sources posed a problem for residents for weeks. Many Floridians were residing in shelters without knowing what had happened to their homes. Years of rebuilding faced the state.

Hurricane Charley was the first significant storm of the 2004 season, and it was the strongest one since Hurricane Andrew. Charley intensified to a Category 4 (5 is the highest) when it came ashore. In early September, Hurricane Frances made its first landfall. Frances's second landfall produced powerful storm surges. Along with the heavy rain from Frances, numerous tornadoes formed throughout the state.

Hurricane Ivan was developing over the Atlantic on the same day that Frances struck Florida. A Category 3 storm, Ivan packed a potent punch. Growing to the size of the state of Texas, Ivan's storm surge reached over five hundred miles from its point of contact. Just three weeks after Frances, Hurricane Jeanne followed, traversing almost the same route as Frances. Seven inches of rain accompanied the winds of Hurricane Jeanne.

This was the first time since 1886 that four hurricanes impacted one state. The resulting costs of these four hurricanes totaled almost forty billion dollars and ninety fatalities.

The year 2005 did not provide any relief for Florida. Hurricane Dennis came ashore on Santa Rosa Island on July 10th. Creating storm surges of six to seven feet, Dennis also spawned nine tornadoes in Florida. Before Dennis dissipated, the hurricane resulted in fourteen deaths and over 2.5 billion dollars in damage. The next month, as a

Category 1 hurricane, Katrina made landfall on the southeastern coast of Florida. Moving over the Everglades, Katrina gathered strength before attacking Louisiana, eventually turning into a Category 5 hurricane.

Wrapping up the hurricane season was Wilma in October. It made landfall as a Category 3 storm. Southern Florida and the Florida Keys were heavily impacted. Wilma generated ten tornadoes. It resulted in thirty deaths and over nineteen billion dollars in damages to Florida.

A storm of a different kind hit Florida in 2000. The eyes of the world watched as Florida counted and recounted ballots in the presidential election. George W. Bush and Al Gore entered the November election statistically tied. Election polls in Florida on the day and night of the election suggested that Gore had won. After voting in the country closed, major networks declared Al Gore to be the victor and the country's next president.

However, as Florida's results were tabulated, Bush was emerging as the winner. Some networks reversed their call on the winner of the presidency. Even Al Gore called George Bush to concede defeat. More results were tallied, and Gore phoned Bush to recant his concession.

Protestors claiming that Gore had won

The morning after the election, the country did not have a new president. To win the presidency, one of the candidates had to earn Florida's votes in the electoral college. By law in Florida, recounts must occur if the election is close. The first count showed Bush winning the state by less than two thousand votes.

For the next five weeks, counts and recounts happened. Lawyers and lawsuits were plentiful. Novel words were added to the state's and country's vocabulary. Chads, dimpled chads, pregnant chads, and hanging chads became part of everyday conversations. Images of polling officials using magnifying glasses to guess a voter's intentions emerged.

Protestors claiming that Gore was trying to steal Bush's victory

The decision ended up in the Florida Supreme Court, which voted for a recount. Election officers had to determine if a voter's hole punch, or chad, was fully detached or dented. While the recount was progressing, the case was appealed to the US Supreme Court. In a 5-4 vote, the US Supreme Court determined that there were no other valid means of determining the intentions of Florida's voters. The recount would stand. George W. Bush became the country's next president by a margin of 537 votes.

Florida's next storm to weather was the Great Recession. In the years leading up to the recession, real estate and property values rose steadily. This led to more and more people entering the housing market. For Florida, it included snowbirds purchasing a winter residence in addition to full-time Floridians purchasing homes.

However, in December 2007, the housing market's bubble burst. While the boom was occurring, mortgage companies were lending money to almost anyone who applied. Customers who had low credit ratings were being approved for loans, as it was expected that the market would continue to flourish. These mortgages are referred to as subprime, and these mortgages were a contributing factor to the Great Recession.

It all came crashing down. In Florida, unemployment doubled from 4.5 percent to over 11 percent. Florida's gross domestic product plummeted at a rate more than double the rest of the country. Eighty percent of the people who missed one mortgage payment ended up losing their homes. State and local governments drastically reduced their spending since tax revenues declined. More people needed government support, but the government was lacking funds of its own.

Nationally, the Great Recession lasted from 2007 to 2009. Florida felt its impact for longer, in part due to the 2010 Gulf oil spill or the Deepwater Horizon oil spill. An offshore drilling rig leased by BP exploded and collapsed, killing eleven people and eventually releasing over a hundred million gallons of oil. It was the largest oil spill in history, and it occurred in the Gulf of Mexico.

The oil leaked for eighty-seven days before its operators were able to stop the discharge. A total of almost five million barrels of oil had flowed into the Gulf of Mexico by that point. Efforts to contain the distance and amount of oil did lessen the impact. However, extensive damage to marine life and water quality continued for years.

A sign encouraging people to not buy BP gasoline

Around 177 miles of Florida's coastline was negatively impacted by the spill. Oil debris and tar balls reached Florida's shores forty-six days after the explosion. Florida's tourism industry suffered as a result, as did other states (especially Louisiana, which was still rebuilding after the devastating impact of Hurricane Katrina). Tourist cancellations mounted as news of the spill spread throughout the country. To minimize the number of cancellations, Florida's tourism industry mounted an aggressive advertising campaign. Live videos of the clean beaches were posted on the internet.

Florida's tourism industry accounts for over 21 percent of the state's sales tax revenue. Additionally, almost one million people derive their living from tourists and tourism. Due to the oil spill, Florida lost billions of dollars in revenue. The loss of income from tourism, coupled with the housing market setbacks from subprime lending, lengthened Florida's recovery from the Great Recession.

The negative news for Florida was not yet over. The last Space Shuttle mission from Kennedy Space Center took place in 2011. NASA began working on the Space Shuttle program in 1972. President Richard Nixon declared that NASA would create a space transportation system, and he gave NASA the challenge to develop a vehicle that could shuttle between Earth and space. On April 12th, 1981, the first shuttle mission was launched. All 135 Space Shuttle missions originated from Kennedy Space Center.

Columbia and the other orbiters of the shuttle program were vastly different from any spacecraft that NASA had designed and built. The shuttles were constructed as space transporters, and they looked more like airplanes. Boosters were used to propel the shuttle into space. Upon their return, the shuttles glided onto runways similar to commercial airlines. When the shuttles were on their flight path, they flew at a speed of 17,500 miles per hour. At this speed, the crew experienced a sunrise or sunset every forty-five minutes.

A picture of a space shuttle

The first Space Shuttle, the *Columbia,* flew for two decades and transported dozens of astronauts. As technology evolved, the shuttle was updated. Its twenty-eighth and last mission ended in tragedy. On its final approach, the shuttle burned up on reentry, killing all seven crew members.

Challenger was the second shuttle operated from Cape Canaveral, where Kennedy Space Center is located. On its tenth mission, this shuttle also met with a tragic end. On January 28th, 1986, all seven crew members were killed. Shortly after its launch, the *Challenger* broke apart. Aboard the flight was Christa McAuliffe, the first civilian crew member. She was a teacher, and schools all over the country had tuned in to watch the historic moment only to witness the devastation. The program was halted until 1988 in order to review its safety protocol.

Other orbiters in the Space Shuttle program included *Discovery*, *Atlantis*, and *Endeavour*. In total, five hundred million miles were flown throughout the program's history. The shuttles could transport up to seven astronauts on each mission. Throughout the thirty years of the program, 355 people flew on the shuttles.

Since it was intended as a transportation system, the shuttles performed a variety of missions. It was utilized to release satellites, and numerous experiments were completed on the shuttle itself. Shuttles carried crew members to repair the Hubble Space Telescope and other satellites, and they also worked on the International Space Station.

Through the thirty years of the program, thousands of jobs were created. A mix of skills and positions were needed to create and operate the Space Shuttle program. Engineers, technicians, logistical support, and more moved to the Space Coast (the region around Kennedy Space Center) for their involvement in the program. Support jobs were generated through the new housing built, the services needed by the NASA employees who moved to the area, and the companies who supplied parts to NASA.

The last Space Shuttle to fly was the *Atlantis*, and it launched in July 2011. With four crew members aboard, it flew its thirty-third and final mission. Supplies and parts were delivered to the International Space Station. Its five-million-mile journey concluded at 5:57 a.m. with a safe landing at Kennedy Space Center. *Atlantis* was part of the Space Shuttle fleet for twenty-six years. During its time in service, *Atlantis* navigated 126 million miles, circled Earth over 4,800 times, and stayed in space for 307 days.

Layoffs commenced shortly after the last flight. NASA and jobs that supported NASA employed over forty thousand residents in the area of Kennedy Space Center. Employees for NASA earned almost double the wages of other workers in Brevard County, and the state of Florida derived over four billion dollars in revenue. The last flight of the space shuttle occurred when employment in Florida was already at almost 12 percent.

Kennedy Space Center eliminated 7,500 positions. Indirect jobs that were reduced were double those of the Space Center. Hair salons, movie theaters, and gyms all felt the results of the economic downturn. It would take the area years to rebound.

Conclusion

For over twelve thousand years, people have lived in present-day Florida. The region offered water, food supplies, stones to make tools, and firewood, providing the first settlers a basis to build their societies. The original colonizers evolved and created complex societies as time passed.

When the Europeans found the North American continent in the 1500s, they found thriving tribes of Native Americans. Within two hundred years, the vast majority of the indigenous peoples bordered on extinction. Warfare, European diseases, and enslavement quickly eradicated these societies that had progressed over thousands of years. Remnants of villages, tools, pottery, and mounds provide information about the earliest settlers of the land, and evidence of the past is still being discovered.

Though Florida was not one of the original Thirteen Colonies, its days as a colony mirror the Europeans' struggle for dominance on the North American continent. The competition for wealth and power placed Florida in the center of many battles and shifting allegiances. Spain, Britain, and France all had interests in Florida, as its location and natural resources made it appealing for each.

After the formation of the United States, the new country had the same interests in Florida as the European monarchies. One of Florida's earliest struggles was maintaining a sustainable population. However, once Florida was connected to the United States, the population flourished. Henry Flagler's role in developing Florida's railway system and luxury hotels began its transformation into a tourist destination and desirable place to live.

Today, Orlando, Florida, is one of the most visited United States destinations with over seventy-five million tourists. Annually, over 145 million visitors explore Florida's theme parks, cruise ships, beaches, sports teams, and natural wonders. Almost one hundred billion dollars are spent per year by Florida's visitors. Tourism is Florida's fourth-largest employer—third if you do not include the government. Since many tourists' visits include locations such as the Everglades, protecting and restoring those assets is important.

Welcome to the Sunshine State!

An increasing desire to preserve Florida's historic and cultural resources is demonstrated in the number of laws, regulations, and groups that support preservation. However, there is much work to still be done before more of its history is razed for more development. Florida Forever replaced Preservation 2000 in 1999. The more encompassing program added historical preservation to its scope.

Land, culture, natural resources, and historical treasures are sought for protection under Florida Forever, which remains an important program to Floridians to this day.

Florida is attractive to many United States companies. In addition to the sunshine and outdoor life it provides for employees, Florida offers favorable tax rates. It also has an effective highway system that is continually adapted to meet changing needs. Florida's airports are spread throughout the state, and they are constantly modernized, offering ease of access to the state. Universities and community colleges in Florida have expanded, with over 340,000 students. Its State University System is the second-largest secondary educational system in the country with twelve different schools. Some of these attributes attracted private industries to come back to the Space Coast.

This area is also named the Comeback Coast, as the revival of the space industry has created numerous jobs in the region since NASA's closure of the Space Shuttle program. Just between 2018 and 2019, over seven thousand well-paying jobs were added to the aerospace industry. Just as with the ramifications when the reductions in space-related jobs occurred, other segments of the economy have benefited from this job creation. Launches from Kennedy Space Center have returned, as have the visitors. With new goals of reaching Mars and further exploring the moon, pride and excitement are back. The future of Florida should be exciting to witness.

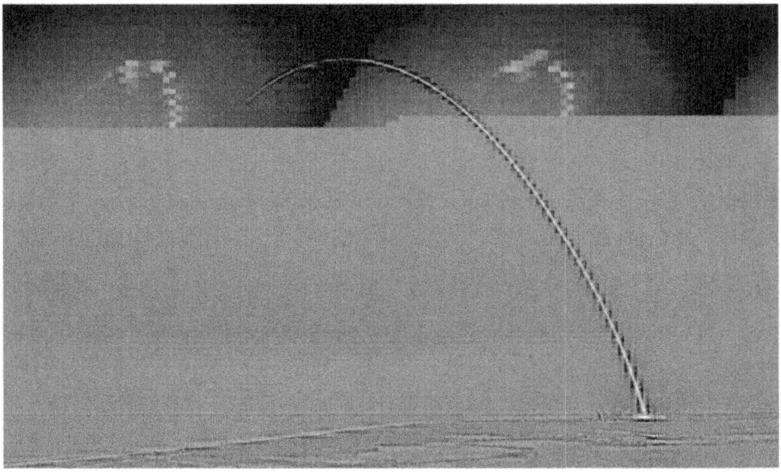

Today, you can do many things in Florida, including watching a rocket launch.

Here's another book by Captivating History that you might like

Free Bonus from Captivating History (Available for a Limited time)

Hi History Lovers!

Now you have a chance to join our exclusive history list so you can get your first history ebook for free as well as discounts and a potential to get more history books for free! Simply visit the link below to join.

Captivatinghistory.com/ebook

Also, make sure to follow us on Facebook, Twitter and Youtube by searching for Captivating History.

Sources

https://dos.myflorida.com/. Date accessed: 11/15-12/15/2021.

http://info.flheritage.com/. Date accessed: 11/15-12/15/2021.

https://dos.myflorida.com/. Date accessed: 11/15-12/15/2021.

https://www.floridahistoryday.com/for-students/finding-primary-sources/. Date accessed: 11/15-12/15/2021.

https://www.noaa.gov/stories/. Date accessed: 11/15-12/15/2021.

www.history.com. Date accessed: 11/15-12/15/2021.

Florida's Eight Regions in Spanish & English. 2005, p9-20.

http://prehistoricflorida.org/indigenous-peoples-of-florida/. Date accessed: 11/15-11/25/2021.

http://www.keyshistory.org/prehistindians.html. Date accessed: 11/15-11/25/2021.

https://www.artnews.com/art-news. Date accessed: 11/15-12/15/2021.

https://www.legendsofamerica.com/, Date accessed: 11/15/2021-12/10/2021.

https://dos.myflorida.com/historical/preservation/great-floridians-program/.

Date accessed: 12/15/2021

https://myfloridahistory.org/. Date accessed: 11/15-12/15/2021.

https://www.battlefields.org/. Date accessed: 11/15-11/28/2021.

https://floridahumanities.org/. Date accessed: 11/15-12/01/2021.

https://fcit.usf.edu/florida/docs/h/hisoffl.htm. Date accessed: 12/01-12/18/2021.

https://visittallahassee.com/civil-rights-timeline/. Date accessed: 12/10/2021.

https://historicspacecraft.com/

https://www.nasa.gov/mission_pages/apollo/missions/index.html.

Date accessed: Dec. 2021

https://www.seminolenationmuseum.org/history/seminole-nation/pre-history/.

Date accessed: 1/1/2022

https://www.exploresouthernhistory.com/westflorida.html. Date accessed: 1/2/2022

https://arthurashe.ucla.edu/2016/07/27/massacre-unveiled-remembering-the-negro-fort/. Date accessed: 1/2/2022

https://www.womenshistory.org/education-resources/biographies/mary-mcleod-bethune. Date accessed: 1/5/2022

Images

https://pixabay.com

https://unsplash.com

https://commons.wikimedia.org

Made in United States
Orlando, FL
14 June 2022

18797919R00075